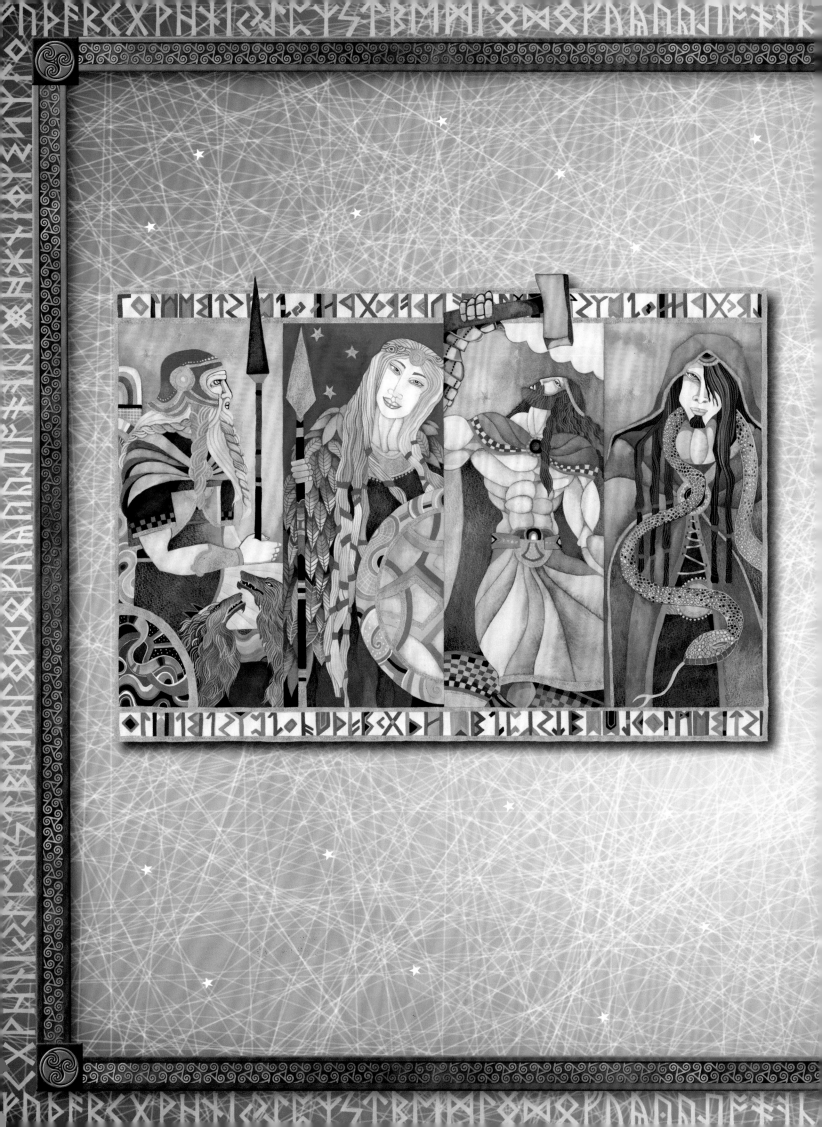

TREASURY OF
NORSE
MYTHOLOGY

STORIES OF INTRIGUE, TRICKERY, LOVE, AND REVENGE

DONNA JO NAPOLI

ILLUSTRATIONS BY CHRISTINA BALIT

NATIONAL
GEOGRAPHIC

WASHINGTON, D.C.

CONTENTS

INTRODUCTION

During the Middle Ages Latin became the language of writing and of much religious storytelling in many lands of Europe. So, for example, in Germany and France people would speak German or French to friends and business associates, but when they wrote books or told Christian stories, they used Latin. The countries in what is today Scandinavia spoke Old Norse, common to all three countries, Norway, Denmark, and Sweden. However, even after Latin writing came to Iceland—which was settled by Norse people— they wrote their own stories in Old Norse, not Latin. In Iceland the tradition of skaldic poetry and song was fundamental to daily culture. People gathered in large halls at any excuse to listen to stories, often because a visiting poet had come to the village. Stories could warm a long cold night, after all. This might well be the reason why some Norse people tenaciously maintained the worldview you will encounter in the stories here until the middle of the 12th century, in opposition to the rising strength of Christianity in neighboring countries.

The Norse stories in many ways reflect the geophysical world the people of Norway and Iceland inhabited. Norway is covered with mountains, the tallest of which are essentially barren—and four are volcanic. Iceland is covered with volcanoes, many of which are active. And both countries have snow and ice in many areas in winter and in some areas even year-round, and each has a long coast lapped by an icy ocean. In such an environment the land and sea themselves must have seemed alive. At any moment the earth might roar, spit fire, and swallow you, or it might shake and an avalanche of snow could smother your homestead. Even a piece of rock, if smacked against a glassy stone, could produce hot sparks that set afire whatever dry twigs were at hand. It's no wonder then that not just living beings had names, but all sorts of objects had names, too. Bridges and halls, trees and swords, inanimate objects of so many kinds had personalities and powers, and it was important to show respect through calling them by name—and never, never to do so frivolously.

The world must have seemed outrageously dangerous; death waited behind any door, and, oh, how savage that death might be. Nevertheless, these people got in boats and braved seas turbulent with storms as they explored and exploited other worlds. The Norse both paid homage to and defied the unknown. The spirit of courage colors their mythology, even as trickery leads to tragedy. And perhaps facing adversity all the time is at least partly the reason why they had a democratic society in which all free men (not women, and not slaves) had a vote—just as all gods had a vote in the assemblies that the major god, Odin, led. Lives depended on decisions made in communal meetings, so it was best to share both the privilege and the responsibility.

Old Norse used letters that don't appear in the modern alphabet for English, such as Þ, which indicates the first sound in *think*; ð, which indicates the first sound in *the*; and æ, which indicates the first sound in *act*. They also added marks above or below vowels to indicate a variety of sounds. While these Old Norse alphabetic symbols are beautiful, I feared that using them here would inhibit you from reading passages aloud. I wouldn't risk robbing you of that joy. So, I have anglicized all proper names here. Further, Norse names often end in *r* because a final *r* can be a nominative case marker, showing that the word is the subject of its sentence. Since English does not use case markings on names, for the sake of consistency, I've chosen to leave out nominative case-marking final *r*'s. Thus, "Óðinn, the Alfaðir of the Æsir," is known here as "Odin, the Allfather of the Aesir." "Þorr, who swings his hammer, Mjölnir," is here "Thor, who swings his hammer, Mjolnir." And so on.

If you would like to know more about Old Norse, please consult a site for the International Phonetic Alphabet (IPA), such as *www.phonetics.ucla.edu/course/chapter1/chapter1.html* or *en.wikipedia.org/wiki/International_Phonetic_Alphabet*. Then use the IPA to help you understand a site on Old Norse, such as *www.omniglot.com/writing/oldnorse.htm*. Please watch the wonderful video there.

ODIN

LOKI

THOR

FREYJA

BALDER

HEL

FREY

KVASIR

IDUNN

HEIMDALL

JORMUNGAND

FRIGG

FENRIR

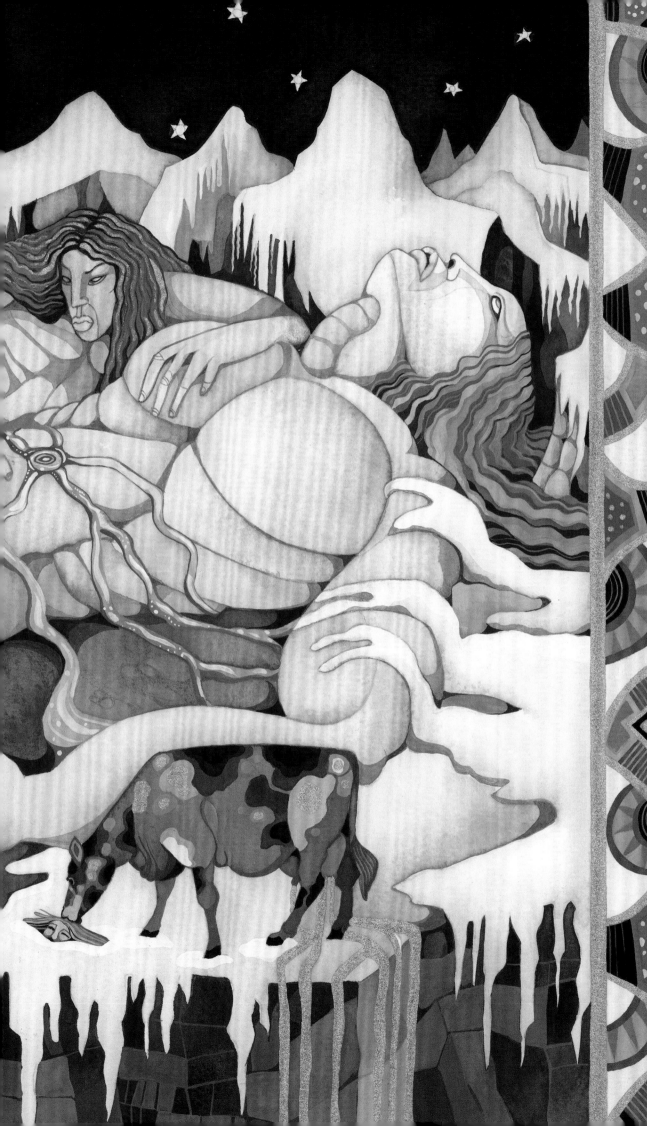

CREATION

The north was frozen—snow and ice, nothing more. It was called Niflheim. It was the embodiment of bleakness.

The south was aflame–ready to consume whatever might come. It was called Muspell. It was the embodiment of insanity.

Between them lay a vast emptiness. It was called Ginnungagap. It waited.

In the midst of the northern realm, water bubbled up—in the spring known as Hvergelmir. From it ran 11 rivers, straight down into the void, filling the northern part of Ginnungagap. The cold rivers slowed and thickened, like icy syrup, but a venomous kind of syrup. One that matched the desolate cries of the haunted winds.

The southern part of Ginnungagap was hot, though. Muspell kept it molten, like lava.

So when the gusts from the northern part met the heaving heat from the southern part, the middle of Ginnungagap grew almost balmy. The icy rivers thawed just enough to drip over that wide middle part.

That was enough: The frost giant Ymir stepped out of those drops. From the sweat of his left armpit grew a frost giant son and daughter. Ymir's feet rubbed together, and another frost giant was born. Ymir's every move, every thought, resulted in more frost giants. And all of them

PREVIOUS PAGES:
The frost giant Ymir emerged from the melting rivers of Ginnungagap. A daughter sprang from his sweaty armpit; a son, from his feet. The sweet-tempered cow Audhumla licked at the ice until she uncovered the head of the first god, Buri.

Heavenly Movements

People used to think the sun and moon crossed the sky. But in 1543 astronomer Nicolaus Copernicus argued that the Earth circles the sun, based on his observations of constellations and a lunar eclipse. Later astronomers Tycho Brahe and Johannes Kepler made astronomical measurements, which led to Kepler's laws of planetary motion around the sun. In 1609 astronomer Galileo Galilei invented the telescope and added support to Copernicus's model based on observations of the planet Venus.

The moon and sun

were spitting mean. What else could they be, given the bitter source of the very liquid in their veins?

The ice of Ginnungagap kept melting as the air grew milder. It formed a cow, a huge good-natured beast, from whose udders spurted four milk rivers. Her name was Audhumla. She stood in the middle of the glistening blocks of salty ice, and like any good cow, she immediately started licking. She licked all day long, until, under her great rasping tongue, hair appeared out of the ice. She licked all the next day, until a whole head appeared. By the evening of the third day, an entire being stood there. He was Buri, the first god.

Buri soon had a son named Bor, and Bor married the daughter of a frost giant and fathered three sons, the grandchildren of Buri: Odin and Vili and Ve.

Now the trouble began: The sons of Bor and the gang of frost giants hated each other. Inevitably, perhaps, for the world was still such an inhospitable place, ice on one side, fire on the other, that hate found a natural home there. Bor's sons killed Ymir.

The blood of that ancient frost giant surged out over Ginnungagap and drowned all the other frost giants—all but two: Bergelmir and his wife. They got in their boat and let the gory current carry them where it would.

But now the sons of Bor found themselves with this enormous corpse, and they recognized the possibilities: Life could come from death. That could be the circle of things. So they used every part of the slain Ymir to create many worlds. His blood made seas and lakes. His flesh made earth. His bones formed mountains. His teeth became rocks and pebbles.

Ymir's hollowed-out skull made the sky, and the three sons of Bor took the maggots crawling in Ymir's rotted carcass and created small creatures called dwarfs. They set a dwarf under each of the four corners of this skull-sky to hold it up, arching over the earth. One dwarf was called Nordri—North; one, Austri—East; one, Sudri—South; one, Vestri—West. The other dwarfs ran off to live in the rocky caves. They became skilled craftsmen. It was they who wrought the decorative treasures of the gods.

The three sons of Bor killed the frost giant Ymir and used his body parts to create worlds and the objects within those worlds. From his skull they made the sky.

But there was still more of Ymir's body to exploit. The sons of Bor threw his brains up into the sky to form clouds. They stole embers from Muspell and created the sun and moon, and from the sparks they made all the many stars.

With Ymir's eyebrows they made a wall to keep out the giants. The land outside that wall was called Jotunheim, and the only two giants left alive settled there. The land inside that wall was called Midgard.

So now the land of Midgard was protected from giants,

from ice, from fire, and it had sweet air above. It grew green with leeks and fragrant clover. Trees shot up, spruce and elm and ash. The gods, who had grown in number, wandered over this land. From two pieces of driftwood on the seashore, three gods created a man and a woman, the first humans. Odin put his mouth to theirs and gave them Ond—Breath—so they could live and love. Hoenir gave them Od—Mind—so they could understand and laugh. Lodur gave them La—Sense—so they could appreciate beauty. And that lone man, Ask, and that lone woman, Embla, set about having children to populate the land of Midgard.

Meanwhile, the giants were having children, too. One giant woman had raven black hair and skin the hue of tree bark. To touch her was to shiver. Her name was Night. She had a son with hair that looked like the tips of the flames in Muspell and skin the color of Audhumla's milk. To touch him was to smile. His name was Day. Their contrast fascinated Odin—he couldn't

resist; he set Night and her son Day in two chariots that race across the sky, the one after the other. Night's chariot horse is Hrimfaxi, with frost clumped in his mane. Day's chariot horse is Skinfaxi, with sparkles flying from his mane.

A human living in Midgard had children that were stunningly beautiful, as beautiful as anything the gods had created. He called his daughter Sun and his son Moon. Such audacity was a grave mistake. In fury, the sons of Bor snatched them and made Sun guide the chariot of Day and Moon guide the chariot of Night. The chariots are always in a hurry because each is chased by a savage wolf, sons of a giantess witch who lives in Ironwood Forest to the east of Midgard. The wolf Hati Hrodvitnisson goes after Moon—he will run Moon down in the end, at the cosmic battle of Ragnarok. The wolf Skoll snaps and growls behind Sun. In the end, he will catch her, too.

That's how it all began. That's how it all will end.

THE COSMOS

The cosmos consisted of separate worlds arranged on three levels. In the middle level many creatures made a home. Humans had Midgard. Frost giants had Jotunheim.

The gods needed a home, too. Now up on the top level of the cosmos there was only one world at this point: Alfheim. That's where the light elves lived, happy souls. So the sons of Bor chose to build a world for the gods up there, beside Alfheim. They named the world of the gods Asgard. It had spreading green meadows and splendid meeting halls.

By now the deities had multiplied and they had welcomed into their group various other creatures, friendly giants and elves. Odin was looked at as the father god; they called him Allfather. And the deities of this huge family called themselves the Aesir. They built a flaming rainbow bridge called Bifrost that spanned the distance from Midgard up to Asgard. Between Bifrost's flames and the high rock wall that surrounded the world, others were blocked from invading Asgard. But Bifrost's flames welcomed the Aesir; they simply shimmered in three colors under the gods' galloping horses as they passed across into their new dwelling.

The Aesir built a hall from a single slab of gold, called Gladsheim, and it served as their court. They built a hall specifically for the goddesses, called Vingolf. They built a home with a forge and made hammers, tongs, anvils, all

PREVIOUS PAGES: One-eyed Odin presides over Asgard, the world of the Aesir gods, as a guardian father—the Allfather. A flaming bridge, Bifrost, leads from Midgard, the world of the humans, up past the wall that surrounds Asgard.

manner of tools, and furnished it well with goods of stone and wood and metal. The dishes they ate from were gold.

Odin built his own hall, Valaskjalf, and thatched it with sheer silver. He sat there on a high seat called Hlidskjalf, from which he could look out over all the worlds in the cosmos.

Those worlds now included one more: Vanaheim. The gods had split into two groups, the Aesir, who inhabited Asgard, and the Vanir, who lived in Vanaheim. The Aesir saw themselves as the true rulers of the cosmos. Given that attitude, it was no surprise that the feelings between the Aesir and the Vanir were less than friendly. So Odin watched Vanaheim with special care.

Odin ruled from his high seat, a helmet on his head and a raven on each shoulder. At his feet crouched two wolves,

Center of the Cosmos

An ash tree stands in a field.

The center of the Norse cosmos was an ash tree named Yggdrasil (see page 22), a legend that may have its origin in the Arctic Sami people. They build a house with hide stretched across poles. So, a tree was the center of the home. That Yggdrasil was an ash tree makes sense. Ash resists splitting, so it makes good bows and tool handles. It's springy, so it makes good mountain-walking sticks. It burns well, even when freshly cut. And it's very hard, so it doesn't wear out quickly.

Geri and Freki, ravenous beasts who ate whatever food Odin dropped for them, which was abundant, since Odin himself lived only on wine. But these two wolves were also rumored to feed on nasty things—maybe even the corpses of men.

And there were many corpses to feed on, for humans were more fragile than gods. On the third and lowest level of the cosmos was the realm of the dead. It took nine days to ride northward and downward from Midgard to get there. It was the deep and frozen northern land of Niflheim. A hateful monster presided there, all pink down to her hips and then greenish black and decayed from hip to toes, with a huge, bloody-muzzled dog, Garm, baying at her side. She went by the name Hel, and many called her realm by her name. In those days, to die was to go to Hel.

Beyond these six worlds, there were three more, whose locations are murky, as is that of Vanaheim. Fire giants dwelled in the smoky landscape Muspell. Dwarfs had the mountain caves in the land called Nidavellir. Near them was Svartalfheim, the land of the dark elves. They were crabby, mysterious beings, as different from the light elves as the moon is from the sun.

Rising up through the center of it all was a mighty ash tree called Yggdrasil. Its branches shaded all the nine worlds, and it dripped a

The ash tree Yggdrasil rose in the middle level of the cosmos, but it stretched its roots down to the bottom level and its branches up into the top level, making a whole that would stand strong only so long as the tree stood strong.

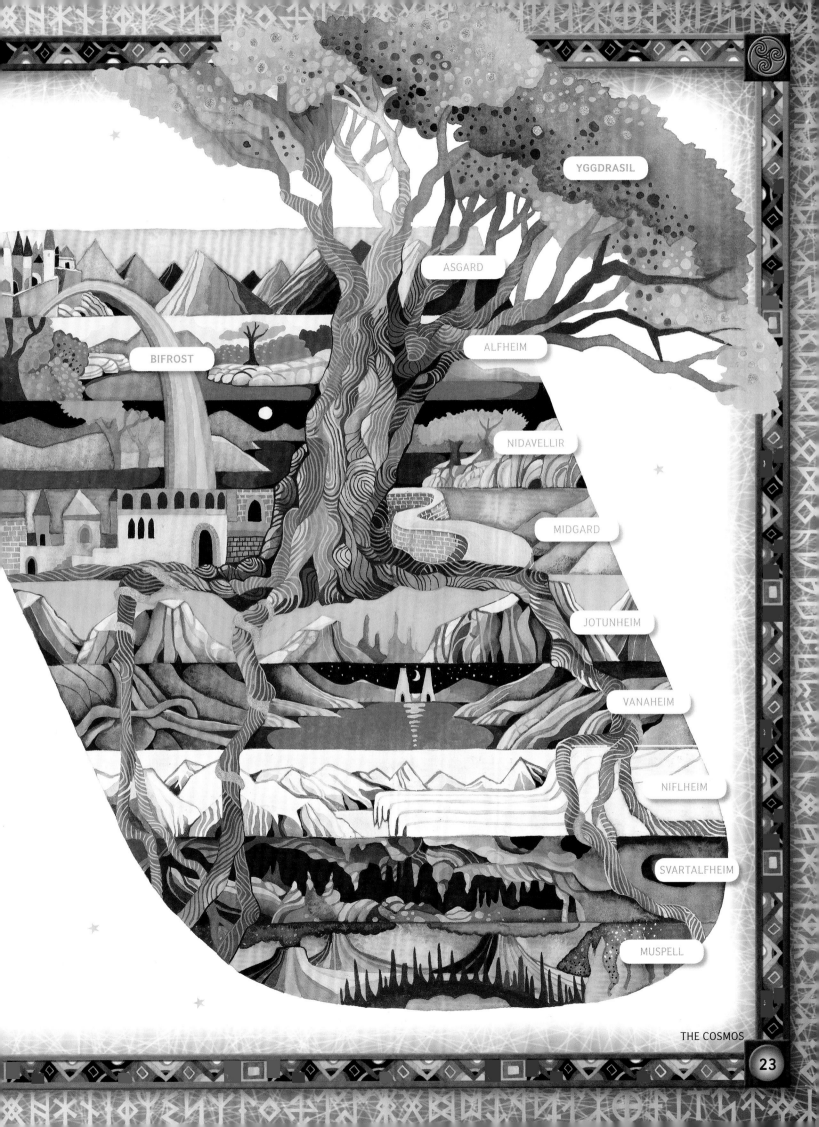

YGGDRASIL

ASGARD

BIFROST

ALFHEIM

NIDAVELLIR

MIDGARD

JOTUNHEIM

VANAHEIM

NIFLHEIM

SVARTALFHEIM

MUSPELL

THE COSMOS

All the animals romping and feeding on Yggdrasil seem ordinary except for the dragon Nidhogg. Serpentine dragons slither through the Norse myths, embodiments of the lurking dangers of the natural world.

sugary dew that swarms of bees made honey from—the very first honeydew. Three gigantic roots held it up, one that went through low Niflheim, one that went through Jotunheim on the middle level, and one that went through the highest land, Asgard. Gnawing at the cold root in Niflheim was the dragon Nidhogg. The squirrel known as Ratatosk ran up and down Yggdrasil, carrying words of envy and insult between the dragon below and the eagle that circled its talons around the tree's limbs. Four stags leaped through the highest boughs,

nibbling at the leaves. And a goat called Heidrun chewed on its tender shoots. Yggdrasil groaned in agony, yet stood tall with nobility. It was the noblest of trees. It looked out over everything, and the knowledge of the worlds seeped into it.

With all this abuse, surely the magnificent tree would have withered but for the efforts of three Norns. Norns were giantesses who ruled the destinies of humans. There were many of them, some malevolent, some beneficent. They were the ones responsible for one man's son dying of illness and another's surviving that same illness,

Three special Norns tended Yggdrasil. They gave the tree water from a sacred spring and coated its bark with that spring's clay to keep it from decaying with age.

for one woman perishing in her first childbirth and another producing a dozen offspring and still planting and plowing with strength. They were present at the birth of every child and no one could escape the fate they assigned. Whenever anything strange happened, anything weird, everyone knew it was the work of the Norns. Three of these Norns, lovely maidens all, took to caring for Yggdrasil. One was Urd—Fate. One was Verdandi—Being. One was Skuld—Necessity. They watered Yggdrasil daily with the purest water from the sacred spring of destiny, and they whitened the bark with clay from that very spring, to make it shine as clean and new as the lining of an eggshell and to protect it from rot and decay.

Yggdrasil served every kind of creature in every world of the cosmos. This most central tree made a whole of the cosmos, and so it was the most sacred place of all. Everyone knew that when Yggdrasil finally would shake, everyone would curl in fear, for the end of everything as we know it would be at hand. Indeed, that may be why the hideous dragon Nidhogg tormented the tree—to put an end to what otherwise would be eternal. In the meantime, though, just the sight of Yggdrasil calmed the most frantic heart.

THE GODS CLASH

The two groups of gods living in the cosmos didn't trust each other much. Rather, they were wary to the extreme. One day a witch named Gullveig, who lived with the Vanir in Vanaheim, visited the Aesir, living in Asgard. No one's really sure why, but Gullveig walked into Odin's hall and blathered about gold, about how it glistened and how much she loved it. The Aesir listened with growing disdain and finally did the unforgivable: They jammed spears into her everywhere. Then they tossed her into a fire and burned her to death. All she had done was annoy them with her incessant talk, and just look what they did to her!

But Gullveig stepped right back out of the flames, alive and whole. A second time they threw her in, and a second time she stepped back out. And yet a third time. By that point the astonished Aesir realized this witch had powers beyond anything they'd dreamed of, so they moved aside and let her wander wherever she wished in the halls of Asgard. Troublemakers followed her; the more wicked the followers, the more they admired Gullveig. Word got back to the Vanir of how dreadfully the Aesir had treated Gullveig. Vengeance seemed a duty; they prepared for war.

From his high seat in Valaskjalf, Odin saw what was happening over in Vanaheim. He saw them sharpening spearheads and polishing shields. So, he prepared a preemptive

PREVIOUS PAGES:
The Aesir mistreated the old witch Gullveig, who lived with the Vanir. In revenge, the Vanir prepared to attack. But the Aesir made a preemptive attack. The bloody battle went on for eons.

Berserkers

In the Icelandic sagas Odin's warriors put on animal fur coverings. Wolf fur let them fight with trickery. Bear fur let them wrestle with strength. Their fighting bordered on insanity; they went berserk (*ber* was the Old Norse word for "bear"). The Vikings, likewise, were known for their ferocious frenzy in battle. These "berserkers" terrorized much of northern Europe in the late 700s until the early 900s, but their more mild Norse compatriots settled peacefully throughout the same area.

Odin, Thor, and Frey on a Viking tapestry

strike, and the Aesir cast the first spear. But the Vanir were already surging forward on their mounts, trampling the fields between the two worlds.

The battle went on and on. That's how battles between gods are. Both sides are immensely powerful, after all. But the longer the battle endured, the clearer it became to all that a victor was unlikely. The gods wearied of the futility of this dreary war. Finally, the leaders of the Vanir and the Aesir sat down to hash things out. They couldn't agree on almost anything, but they wanted so much just to end that plague of war that they drew up a truce. And to show their sincerity, they exchanged hostages: Two from each group would go to live with the other group.

The Vanir sent the very wealthy god Njord and his son Frey to Asgard. Frey's twin sister, Freyja, and Kvasir, the wisest

Vanir, accompanied those two on their journey and ended up staying there. The Aesir welcomed them honorably. Njord and Frey were appointed high priests to preside over sacrifices. Freyja became a sacrificial priestess, and she taught the gods all the spiritual, medical, and magical knowledge that she had, which was considerable.

The Aesir, for their part, sent Hoenir and Mimir to Vanaheim. Hoenir was strong and big; he certainly looked like he'd make a fine leader. And Mimir, though he was a giant, was considered the wisest Aesir—definitely comparable to Kvasir. All seemed good to the Vanir. They put Hoenir in a position of power and Mimir stood to his right and advised him. Together they made shrewd decisions. But if Mimir left Hoenir's side, the tall and handsome Hoenir turned silent. When asked a question, he refused to speak. The Vanir felt cheated. In fury, they cut off Mimir's head and sent it back to Odin.

Why they cut off poor Mimir's head because of closed-mouthed Hoenir is unfathomable. Gods had their own ways of doing things.

Odin was bereft, for Mimir had been a fine and true friend. He held that severed head in his arms and crooned to it. Then he coated it with herbs that would retard decay and sang magic incantations over it. The head of Mimir regained its power of speech and thenceforth became a font of wisdom for Odin.

And thus the first war in the cosmos began and ended. But it wasn't the last. Humans waged war often. And the gods treated the corpses of men who died in battle very well. They didn't go to Hel. No, no. Half of them went to Asgard to live in a special hall called Valhalla, where spear shafts served as rafters and the roof was thatched with shields. At the western door lurked a wolf with an eagle hovering overhead. To arrive in Valhalla, the fallen warriors had to cross a large, noisy river. Once there, Odin welcomed them heartily. He had straw strewn on the benches in the hall to make them comfortable; he had all the goblets polished, for he already foresaw needing these warriors. Someday, he knew, there would be a final great battle among gods, humans, monsters, giants, everyone—the all-consuming Ragnarok. Warriors would be invaluable.

The Aesir sent the wise giant Mimir to their rival gods, the Vanir, in an exchange. But the Vanir got angry and cut off poor Mimir's head. Odin grieved for his lost friend.

The Valkyries flew on their horses over battle-fields and chose the best fallen warriors to bring back to Valhalla. The warriors feasted and practiced their martial arts there, preparing for the great battle of Ragnarok that would come someday.

Odin's helper maids, the Valkyries, put on silver helmets from which their golden hair flowed out and red corselet armor that emphasized their beautiful bodies, and they rode on white horses through the air over the battlefields below. They must have appeared both terrifying and alluring to the sweaty, exhausted men as they lay dying. The Valkyries carried the chosen dead up to Valhalla.

And what a fine routine met these warriors there in Valhalla. Every night they feasted on over-flowing platters of pork from the beast Saehrimnir, roasted in the cauldron Eldhrimnir by the soot-covered cook Andhrimnir. They drank never ending mead that came from the udders of the goat Heidrun, the one that ate the tender shoots of the tree Yggdrasil. Every day they battled together, and those who fell in these heavenly battles simply rose again at the end of the day and marched through the 540 doors of the hall to join the feast anew, since everything regenerated of its own accord.

The other half of the dead on the battlefield were gathered up by the priestess Freyja, the Vanir goddess who had taught everyone in Asgard so much about the wonders of the cosmos. She brought them to her heavenly field called Folkvang, where they, too, were groomed for the final battle, Ragnarok.

It's as though right from the beginning of time everyone was preparing for the end of it all.

ODIN'S QUEST

O din was viewed as harsh and severe. And the one he was most severe with was himself.

When Odin sat on his high seat, Hlidskjalf, he could look out over the cosmos and see a great deal. But not everything. *Hmmm.* What was going on behind that ridge over there in the land of the dark elves? Who was whispering what under that root of Yggdrasil in Hel? His throat was parched with the yearning for knowledge. So he relied on the two ravens that perched on his shoulders: Huginn (Thought) and Muninn (Memory). They flew off in the morning to investigate the nine worlds with their sharp eyes. At night they returned to Odin and told him all that they had witnessed.

Still, it wasn't enough. Odin's mind was greedy; knowledge tasted good, but wisdom, ah, that would taste far better.

By this time there were ten major gods in the cosmos beyond Odin (and before too long, there would be two more). Eight of them were Aesir: Odin's sons Thor, Balder,

PREVIOUS PAGES: From his throne, Odin could view all nine worlds. Still, he sent out his two ravens to patrol for him and come back with details about happenings in those corners of the cosmos that his eye couldn't reach.

Tyr, Heimdall, Hod, and Vidar, plus his grandsons Forseti (son of Balder) and Ull (stepson of Thor). The other two major gods lived among the Aesir, but they had come originally from the Vanir: Njord and Frey. Each day Odin and these ten gods rode their horses over Bifrost, the flaming bridge, to that root of the spreading ash tree Yggdrasil that extended to heaven. Beneath that root was the sacred well Urdarbrunn, where the spring of destiny bubbled up. The gods held their assemblies right there. They made decisions that upheld righteousness and justice, and that protected humans against giants and dwarfs and dark elves. As they sat there, Odin watched two swans swimming with a sense of peace he'd never experienced, and he watched the three lovely Norns sprinkle the sacred tree from the spring of destiny and coat its wounds with a clay salve from the well Urdarbrunn. In this watery ritual he recognized something

Odin and the other gods living in Asgard rode their horses every day over the burning bridge, Bifrost. On the other side was the grand ash tree Yggdrasil and the sacred well of destiny.

mystical, beyond reason, something that renewed the everlasting tree's strength, something that gave those swans equanimity. Water did it—water had that unnamed something that could elevate one to an ever greater strength.

That's when Odin took a closer look at the giant Mimir. Mimir was but a head at this point, severed from his body by the Vanir. But he was still the wisest one in all Asgard. Under another root of Yggdrasil, the one that stretched into the frost giants' world, Jotunheim, was a well that Mimir guarded, and so it was called Mimisbrunn. Mimir drank from this well each day. Aha! The well was the source of Mimir's wisdom! Odin had to have at that well.

And so Odin made a deal with Mimir: an eye for a single draught of that well water. Such a high price, this extreme self-mutilation. But what good was an eye that couldn't fathom what it saw? Odin willingly scooped it from his own skull and hid it. He fashioned a drinking horn from dragon skin, dipped it into the well, and opened his mouth wide. The cool water sloshed down his throat and radiated throughout his essence. Yes, Odin knew more now, much more; he understood, he was wise. But, alas, he now knew that the highest wisdom of all—that of clairvoyance—was yet to be attained.

And where else to attain it than from the sacred tree Yggdrasil itself? Odin pierced himself with his spear Gungnir, perhaps so that he could come close to understanding the pain the tree experienced from its daily wounds. Then he hanged himself from a high bough. For nine long days and nine long nights, he swung there. He allowed no one to ease his suffering—not a drop of water passed his lips. In this delirious state, near death, he saw below him runes. He knew runes; some were carved on the tip of Gungnir—mysterious letters. But now those letters formed in the tree roots and they yielded their meanings to him and taught him nine precious songs and magic charms and the art of poetry. He looked out at the nine worlds in a new way. He shuddered at the knowledge he now embodied—at the miseries that lay ahead, at the deeds that lay behind, at all the difficulties of getting from day to day in a decent way.

Healing Waters

Holy water in the Hindu Tirta Empul Temple in Bali

Sacred wells, rivers, and springs appear in many religions, including those of several indigenous people of the Americas, ancient Rome, and India, as well as Christianity. Likewise, sacred words—here in the form of runes, those mysterious letters that took wisdom to decipher—come up repeatedly. Both are associated with the ability to heal, and, sometimes, to destroy. The Norse poem "Hávamál" claims that runic words heal better than leeches, a hint that old Norse medicine was fighting against the newer Christian methods.

Odin proclaimed:

Cattle die, kinsmen die,
The self must also die;
but glory never dies,
for the man who is able to achieve it.

Odin chose to hang himself from Yggdrasil for nine days and nights in his quest for wisdom. He was rewarded with a vision of runes that granted him knowledge of nine magic songs, charms, and poetry.

Odin determined to achieve glory. In this new state he could connect his own ancestry among the giants to the present race of gods, and with that connection he made a whole of the cosmos. To each its time, its place. Everything fit.

Odin, the clairvoyant, now conversed with everyone. People made human sacrifices to the mighty god. They hanged men from trees and pierced them with spears—mimicking the passion of Odin dangling from Yggdrasil those nine days. Who

were these hanged men? Some were dying of disease, and so they dedicated themselves to Odin, to end their lives in the glory of talking with the highest god. Others chose to avoid a natural death by embracing this ceremonial one. And while the men hung there, Odin came to talk with them, to glean what they might know of this life and this death. Odin found solace and pleasure in these shared words. He was proud to be god of the gallows, for dying men told truths.

Odin engaged in this same kind of intimate talk with those fallen on the battlefield. Dead men revealed mysteries—this was an extra advantage of surrounding himself with warriors for the huge war ahead, the one that would come eventually, the dreaded Ragnarok.

Odin thus put his quest for information and, ultimately, understanding of that information before all else. A harsh choice, indeed.

LOKI'S MONSTROUS CHILDREN

LOKI'S MONSTROUS CHILDREN

Loki made everyone edgy.

Loki was the son of the giant Farbauti and the goddess Laufey. Several gods took giantesses as wives, and their offspring did fine. But it was taboo for a goddess to take a giant as a husband; thus, Loki was born with a giant (so to speak) strike against him. But at one point he and Odin mixed blood and thus became blood brothers. Odin, in fact, promised that he would always share drink with Loki. This meant that Loki was counted among the Aesir.

From the start, Loki was spiteful, and that spirit proved to be inheritable. Hapless wives bore him wretched children, three notable for their evilness: the chaos monsters, children by the frost giantess Angrboda. The first was the vicious wolf Fenrir; the second, the serpent Jormungand; and the third, the horrible hag Hel. At first, the children lived with their

PREVIOUS PAGES:
Loki had many offspring, but three were horrendous: the wolf Fenrir, fated to kill Odin in the battle Ragnarok; the serpent Jormungand, whose venom would kill Thor in that battle; and hungry Hel, who would keep Odin's son, Balder, prisoner.

Tricksters and Sneaks

Tricksters appear in many traditions. Some native tribes of North America have Coyote, a well-known prankster, but he reveals people's weaknesses, so he's listened to. The Greek god Hermes was a liar and thief, yet he was eloquent and could convince anyone of anything. Coyote, Hermes, and Loki are shape-shifters. But Coyote is neither good nor evil, Hermes is simply an annoyance, and Loki is wicked. Both Odin and Thor seek Loki out sometimes, however, to use his ability to deceive for good goals.

A Native American rock painting, possibly of Coyote

mother in Jotunheim. But everyone in Asgard knew they were destined to cause cosmic misery eventually. The gods couldn't kill these children—for no one can interfere with fate. But they wanted to be rid of them in the meantime. So the one-eyed Odin had a band of gods sneak into Jotunheim one night and gag and bind the giantess Angrboda and kidnap the children.

Odin decided the wolf Fenrir should live in Asgard, perhaps so he could keep an eye on him. After all, Fenrir was destined to kill Odin at the final battle of Ragnarok. The inhabitants of Asgard were not delighted with the prospect of this beast living among them. The only one who dared get close enough to the wolf to feed him was Odin's son Tyr, whose mother was a giantess and who was bolder than others—a true god of war. Still, as Fenrir grew, fear of him grew until people wanted to

The wolf Fenrir was the son of Loki and a vicious, frightful creature. Odin had him bound in chains and brought to Asgard. But it was hard to capture him: The god Tyr lost his right hand in doing it.

LOKI'S MONSTROUS CHILDREN

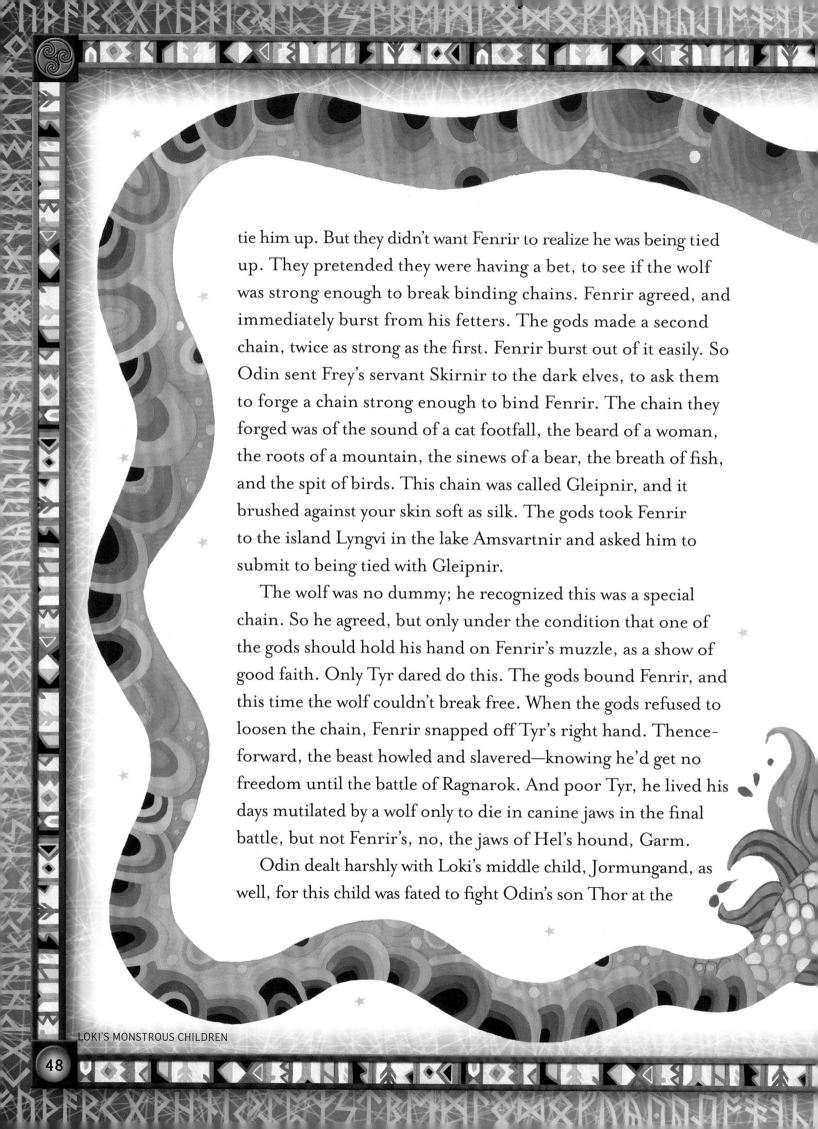

tie him up. But they didn't want Fenrir to realize he was being tied up. They pretended they were having a bet, to see if the wolf was strong enough to break binding chains. Fenrir agreed, and immediately burst from his fetters. The gods made a second chain, twice as strong as the first. Fenrir burst out of it easily. So Odin sent Frey's servant Skirnir to the dark elves, to ask them to forge a chain strong enough to bind Fenrir. The chain they forged was of the sound of a cat footfall, the beard of a woman, the roots of a mountain, the sinews of a bear, the breath of fish, and the spit of birds. This chain was called Gleipnir, and it brushed against your skin soft as silk. The gods took Fenrir to the island Lyngvi in the lake Amsvartnir and asked him to submit to being tied with Gleipnir.

The wolf was no dummy; he recognized this was a special chain. So he agreed, but only under the condition that one of the gods should hold his hand on Fenrir's muzzle, as a show of good faith. Only Tyr dared do this. The gods bound Fenrir, and this time the wolf couldn't break free. When the gods refused to loosen the chain, Fenrir snapped off Tyr's right hand. Thenceforward, the beast howled and slavered—knowing he'd get no freedom until the battle of Ragnarok. And poor Tyr, he lived his days mutilated by a wolf only to die in canine jaws in the final battle, but not Fenrir's, no, the jaws of Hel's hound, Garm.

Odin dealt harshly with Loki's middle child, Jormungand, as well, for this child was fated to fight Odin's son Thor at the

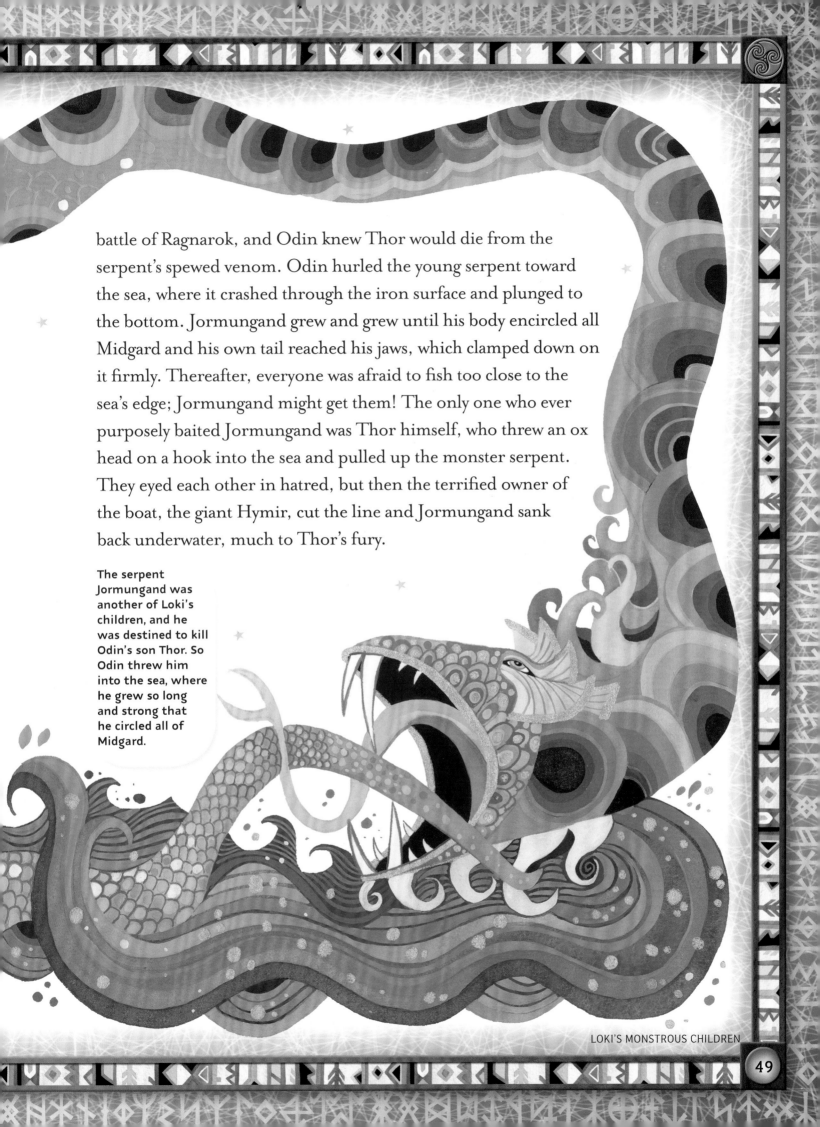

battle of Ragnarok, and Odin knew Thor would die from the serpent's spewed venom. Odin hurled the young serpent toward the sea, where it crashed through the iron surface and plunged to the bottom. Jormungand grew and grew until his body encircled all Midgard and his own tail reached his jaws, which clamped down on it firmly. Thereafter, everyone was afraid to fish too close to the sea's edge; Jormungand might get them! The only one who ever purposely baited Jormungand was Thor himself, who threw an ox head on a hook into the sea and pulled up the monster serpent. They eyed each other in hatred, but then the terrified owner of the boat, the giant Hymir, cut the line and Jormungand sank back underwater, much to Thor's fury.

The serpent Jormungand was another of Loki's children, and he was destined to kill Odin's son Thor. So Odin threw him into the sea, where he grew so long and strong that he circled all of Midgard.

Loki's only daughter was Hel, the spiteful, sour mistress of the underworld. She gathered all the dead who were not warriors—just the ordinary dead—into her cold, joyless realm and held on to them till the end of the world.

As for Loki's third child by Angrboda, Odin banished her to the depths of Niflheim. So Loki's daughter, Hel, was none other than the mistress of the underworld, half alive and half dead. She received all those who died other than in battle—the ones who grew old and feeble, the ones who withered from disease, and all the monsters, animals, giants, and dwarfs. She did that job with a sour taste in her mouth, but never with remorse. She was greedy for prey. Her dish was named Hungr—Hunger; her knife, Sult— Famine; her couch, Kor—Sickbed; and the curtains that surrounded the couch, Blikjandabol—Glimmering Mischance. Once anyone entered her world, she was loath to let them leave. At the start of Ragnarok, her sooty-red cock would crow the announcement of doom.

Loki did many wretched deeds, but his worst involved the assistance of his daughter, Hel. That full story will come

later. Through a perverse trick, Loki caused the death of two of Odin's sons, and Hel made sure they remained in her frozen realm until the terrible battle of Ragnarok. The hearts of the gods were wrenched.

The gods had their revenge on Loki … but that also is another story.

The death of Odin's children is the saddest moment in the gods' history, made even sadder by the fact that the wise Odin was clairvoyant. Remember? That father of the two doomed sons knew these deaths were coming, just as he knew that the destruction of the cosmos was coming. And there was nothing at all he could do to prevent it. In everything Odin did, every breath, every step, he carried with him the knowledge that all of us are helpless in one way or another, even the god known as Allfather. Maybe that tragedy is, after all, the iron nugget of wisdom.

WAGERS & TREASURES

WAGERS & TREASURES

Loki was known as the trickster god and a lot of his trickery smacked of malice, right from the start. The god Thor had a wife named Sif with a face so lovely men and gods were constantly longing for her. But even better was the hair that framed that face—long curling locks the color of sunlight and as thick and rich as summer wheat. One night, when Loki was bored, he climbed into the room where Sif was sleeping and cut off all her hair. It was just as a prank, so he said, but a nasty kind of prank. A woman's beauty was judged by the glory of her hair, and blond hair was the most glorious. Worst of all, only slave girls went with bald heads. When Sif woke, she realized someone had stolen her beauty and humiliated her gravely.

Thor found a shoe outside Sif's window and recognized it as Loki's, lost in Loki's scramble to get away. He grabbed Loki by the neck, ready to crush every bone in his body, but Loki said that only if Thor let him go would Sif's hair grow back. Thor squeezed harder. Loki added that he'd also give astonishing gifts to the gods. Thor released Loki. The trickster god was granted one night and one day to do as he had promised.

Loki went to a group of dwarfs called the Sons of Ivaldi. They were known far and wide to be amazing craftsmen. He persuaded them to make wonders that would fulfill his promises.

PREVIOUS PAGES: Loki cut off Sif's hair and thus robbed her of her glory. Her husband, Thor, was ready to kill Loki, but Loki promised amazing gifts, which he then got the Sons of Ivaldi to make. One gift was the magical ship Skidbladnir.

The Sons of Ivaldi made new hair for Sif from real gold. And this hair was far better than Loki could have hoped, for it grew, like natural hair did, like wheat returning after harvest and winter.

They then built a ship called Skidbladnir. The vessel was huge. All the major and minor Aesir gods could sit in it with all their weapons. Its sails attracted the winds and it went easily wherever it was steered. And the best thing about Skidbladnir was this: The dwarfs had fashioned it of multiple tiny parts, so that when it was hauled onto land, it could be folded up as easily as a scarf and tucked into a pouch to be carried anywhere you wanted.

Next the Sons of Ivaldi crafted a fabulous spear. The master blacksmith dwarf Dvalinn looked on as they worked, giving pointers here and there. The spear's shaft was so perfectly balanced that it struck whatever one aimed at, no matter the

Beautiful Hair

Comb with animal and human heads, pre-Viking Sweden

In medieval Iceland it was illegal for free women to cut their hair short. An unmarried woman could wear her hair loose or braided. A married woman covered her hair with her cap, but her husband knew how lovely it was—just as Thor knew how lovely Sif's long hair was. After the oval brooches that fastened her dress straps, a woman's most treasured possession was her comb, often made from a single piece of whalebone or imported elephant ivory, carved or incised decoratively. Thus, Loki's prank was beastly.

strength or skill of the wielder. They incised runes in its tip and named it Gungnir.

Sif's wig and Skidbladnir and Gungnir were all magical; there's no other word for it. The Sons of Ivaldi strutted in pride at the obvious pleasure on Loki's face. But Loki was surveying them with eyes that were just as keen. Dwarfs were not just powerful, they were prideful. Loki seized the opportunity. He laid a wager with another dwarf, named Brokk, that his brother Sindri could never make objects that matched in wonder the three just made by the Sons of Ivaldi. At stake was Loki's head.

Brokk and Sindri took the bait. Sindri threw a pig hide in the forge and told Brokk to blow the bellows without pause. A fly immediately came along and bit Brokk's arm. Still, Brokk didn't interrupt the puff of the bellows, and when he was done, Sindri lifted from the forge a golden-bristled boar named Gullinbursti who could race through both air and water faster than any horse and whose bristles lit up even the darkest cave. Then Sindri threw gold in the forge and gave Brokk the same instructions. Again the fly came; it bit Brokk on the neck harder than before. But Brokk was steady. Sindri lifted from the forge a gold ring called Draupnir, which every ninth night would drip from the finger of its wearer another eight rings just as splendid.

The brothers Brokk and Sindri were skilled in metalwork. They turned an ordinary pig hide into the golden-bristled boar named Gullinbursti, who was swifter than horses and brighter than flames.

Loki wagered that Brokk and Sindri could not make marvels better than those of the Sons of Ivaldi. The Aesir council had to choose between wonders like the hammer Mjolnir and the spear Gungnir. Loki lost the wager and ran for his life.

Then Sindri put iron in the forge and Brokk worked the bellows. The fly came again. This time it bit Brokk between the eyes and stung his eyelids till blood blinded him. The writhing dwarf couldn't bear it any longer; he swatted the fly away and in the process interrupted the puff of the bellows for just a moment. The result was a hammer named Mjolnir that was powerful enough to level a mountain, would hit anything the thrower aimed at, and would always return to the thrower's fist. But Mjolnir's handle was just a smidgen short because of that wicked fly—and who do you guess might have sent the fly? Or even been the fly himself? But, no matter by what means the wager had been won, Loki claimed victory.

Brokk and Sindri protested, leaving the matter up to the council of the gods to decide. At that council meeting, Loki showered the gods with gifts. He gave to Thor the gold wig for Sif, and to Frey, the ship Skidbladnir. To

Odin he gave the spear Gungnir, which eventually
became the source of much of this god's wisdom, as he
deciphered the runes on Gungnir's tip in the nine long
days and nights he hung from the mighty ash Yggdrasil.
But Brokk offered presents, too. To Frey, he gave the boar
Gullinbursti; to Odin, the ring Draupnir; to Thor, the
hammer Mjolnir. The Aesir council wasn't swayed by
Loki's gifts; it found in favor of Brokk.

Loki ran for his life. Thor seized him, and Brokk was ready
to swing the blade, but Loki argued that the wager was only for
his head, not his neck, and since Brokk couldn't get his head
without cutting his neck, decapitation was impossible. In rage,
the thwarted dwarf sewed Loki's trickster lips together.

Thus did the gods gain their most precious treasures.

But those treasures didn't lessen the hatred toward the
source—Loki. Products of malice never do.

SHAPE-SHIFTERS

Shape-shifters abounded. People were convinced that the visions of beasts and monsters that came to them in dreams were their departed loved ones. And even in ordinary life, you could never be sure who that particularly large bear spying on you might be, or that seal you were dueling with, or even that terribly annoying fly that bit you as you worked at the forge.

The very nature of shape-shifting is deception; thus, it's no surprise that Loki, that disgrace of all beings, had perfected the art of shape-shifting. And sometimes he used it to the advantage of the Aesir. This may well be why some of the gods, especially Thor, enjoyed his company.

In the battle between the Aesir and the Vanir, the stone wall around Asgard was reduced to rubble. The gods wanted it rebuilt, but the task was onerous and no one stepped forward to do it.

No one, that is, until the mason came. He rode into town alone on a fine stallion, and the god Heimdall, who guarded the entrance to this world, stopped him. "What do you want?"

"I have a proposal for the gods," said the mason.

So the gods and goddesses gathered in the hall Gladsheim and Odin said, "Well?"

"I'll rebuild your wall," said the mason. "Stronger and higher than before. No one will be able to breach it. Not even the strongest, tallest frost giants. And I'll do

PREVIOUS PAGES: A rock giant came disguised as a mason to repair Asgard's wall, which had been damaged in the war with the Vanir. His stallion helped him. What he wanted as pay was the sun, the moon, and Freyja as his wife.

A Sacred Transport

In Norse culture, particularly in Iceland, horses were seen as having a dual nature: They were domesticated animals used for riding and carrying burdens, but they also were seen as a typical transport to the underworld in Norse mythology—a bridge between the world of the living and the world of the dead. Thus, they were sacred, and sometimes they were buried with their owners at funerals. This stone carving shows Sleipnir, the eight-legged horse Odin rode.

Picture stone of Sleipnir, from Gotland, Sweden, ninth century

it in just eighteen months." He paused.

Odin recognized the significance of that pause. "Under the condition …?"

"… that Freyja becomes my wife."

Freyja felt a bolt shoot through her. The wife of a human? Never! She was so furious, her private hall Sessrumnir shook.

Shouts of derision came from every direction.

Odin pointed past the mason. "Get out of here!"

"I want the sun and the moon, as well," said the mason. "The three of them: Freyja, the sun, the moon. That's all. That'll do."

Pandemonium broke out.

But a sharp, loud voice pierced all. "Wait a minute." It was Loki. "Let's think it over, at least."

So the mason left, while the gods remained there to hash it out. Freyja wept tears of gold, for that was her habit. Others scorned Loki.

"It's impossible to build a wall that size in eighteen months," said Heimdall.

"My point precisely," said Loki. "Let's agree to his terms. At the end of eighteen months, he'll have failed to meet his promise. We'll owe him nothing. And we'll have whatever part of the wall he's managed to complete. We win, no matter what."

No one liked the idea, but no one could fault Loki's logic.

Odin summoned the mason back. "Six months. That's all

The mason and his horse were given six months to rebuild the wall that surrounded Asgard. That was far too little time for the enormous job. But the lovesick mason accepted the challenge.

you get. Build the wall and you get Freyja, the sun, and the moon."

"That's too short," said the mason.

"Those are the terms. If it's not complete in six months, you forfeit all."

The mason looked at Freyja googly-eyed. He was drunk on her beauty. "Allow me the aid of my stallion, Svadilfari, and we have a deal."

Odin objected. But Loki's voice again rose high. "Would you turn away from the deal at this point? The horse is small help—and we need a wall."

So the gods agreed and the mason assumed the task. He spread out a net and heaved stones onto it, slabs of enormous weight. Why, this mason's strength rivaled that of Thor, the strongest of the gods. Then the mason harnessed this massive load to his stallion and bellowed. The horse thrust forward with all his might, stamping his hoofs into the rocky earth. He proved stronger even than his master. The two of them worked all night. At dawn, the gods and goddesses were astonished to see so many stones already hauled to the wall site. As the days and weeks and months passed, they watched the wall grow. It was thicker, taller, better than ever. And it was nearly finished. The mason and his stallion were a marvel, and a terror. What would the Aesir do if this builder succeeded?

How could they exist without the light and heat of the sun, the comfort of the moon? And poor Freyja, wed to a brute? She stood in a rising puddle of gold tears and chewed at her wrists. It was all too awful.

Odin called a meeting. Everyone railed at Loki.

But Loki had the solution, of course. He'd make sure the mason didn't finish. One way or another.

To Loki it was clear that the stallion was the answer. Without that horse, the mason could carry at most one boulder up the hillside at a time.

That evening, as the mason led Svadilfari back down to the quarry, a mare stepped forward from the thicket beside the path. Her neck was long and sleek, her mane seemed to float around her, her tail was a stream of stars. She kicked up her heels. Her flanks shimmered.

The stallion simmered.

Off they galloped, him behind her. The mason called after his horse. He shouted till his throat was raw. He cursed.

Svadilfari didn't give a backward glance.

In the morning, when the stallion finally returned, the mason realized that one lost night of work had cost him the whole deal. Anger smoldered within until it burst forth and the mason changed into who he really was—a huge rock giant. The gods and goddesses now lost their tempers; no one could come before them disguised

and hope to get away with it, especially not a giant. It was outrageous! Thor hit the giant in the head with his hammer, Mjolnir. The giant's skull shattered, and he immediately found himself in Niflheim. Several months later, Loki, who hadn't been seen in all that time, returned to Asgard. With a colt at his heels, a colt who had eight legs. Loki had been that alluring mare, and with Svadilfari, he had made the magnificent colt Sleipnir. So Loki was actually the colt's mother.

Odin was smitten with the colt immediately. And what was Loki going to do with a colt, after all? He'd been a dreadful father, and he certainly had no desire to be a mother. So Loki gave Sleipnir to Odin.

Loki shapeshifted into a beautiful mare and lured the mason's stallion away so that the mason would not be able to finish the wall in the allotted time. The mason, who was really a rock giant, burst with anger.

HEIMDALL'S MANY CHILDREN

Remember Heimdall? The mason who came to barter his services in rebuilding the wall around Asgard had to pass by Heimdall before he could talk with the council of the gods. That's because Heimdall guarded entry into the Aesir world. He lived on the cliff Himinbjorg at one end of the flaming rainbow bridge, Bifrost, and he always stayed alert for invaders. Heimdall was a perfect pick as guard for three reasons. His eyesight was so keen he could see across vast distances whether day or night. His hearing was so acute that he could hear grass grow. And he needed even less sleep than a bird.

Heimdall was Odin's son, and his mothers—yes, mothers, for he had nine of them—were giantess sisters, as inseparable as sea waves. How this god came into being is a mystery, but there's no question that he was a most astonishing figure. Odin had teeth that could gnaw through stone, true, but Heimdall's teeth were pure gold. Frey rode the golden-bristled boar, Gullinbursti, true, but Heimdall's horse, Gulltopp, had a gold mane. Thor was huge and red-bearded, true, but Heimdall's skin shone white, like the noon sun.

Heimdall owned the horn Gjallarhorn, which he used for both drinking and sounding. He dipped Gjallarhorn into the well Mimisbrunn, which Mimir guarded, and thus drank himself into wisdom. But he also blew Gjallarhorn to summon gods to a meeting or to warn them of the approach of enemies. It would be Heimdall's job to blow Gjallarhorn to announce the battle of

PREVIOUS PAGES: Heimdall, with his horn, Gjallarhorn, rode his golden-maned horse through the countryside of Midgard. He fathered three sons, each one the progenitor of a whole group of people: the slaves, the peasants, and the rich and royal.

Ragnarok. In that battle, he was fated to fight Loki to the death—both their deaths.

So Heimdall was important to the gods. But he was even more important to other creatures.

One spring day, Heimdall strode across Bifrost all the way to the edge of the deepest sea that surrounded Midgard. He found a rickety hut there and gave the door a firm knock. The door swung open to reveal a smoky, stinky room. An old couple peered squinty-eyed at Heimdall and then welcomed him warily. They were Ai the Great Grandpa and Edda the Great Grandma. Their clothes were threadbare, their walls crumbly. Now, Heimdall was accomplished in the ways of the world and he knew how to put others at ease. He spoke with the old couple as though he'd been friends with them all his life, and before long they urged him to sit

Slave Trade

Frightful Viking ship prow

Heimdall walks across the land visiting people, but the Vikings mostly traveled to other lands in boats, often with frightening prows. Sometimes they stole people, often children and women. They took slaves when they plundered towns and monasteries for gold and silver and they snatched slaves at random from coasts. Scientists have found that around 20 to 25 percent of the males who founded Iceland were of Gaelic ancestry. This tells us that many Vikings raided Ireland and Scotland for wives.

closer to the fire, to warm his hands. In no time at all, they were sharing their meager broth with him. And soon enough all three went to sleep in the same bed with Heimdall in the middle.

Heimdall stayed with Ai and Edda three nights, and then he continued on his travels. But he had left behind something; deep inside Edda was a tiny baby boy, Heimdall's son. When he was born nine months later, his mother called him Thraell the Servant.

Thraell was not the most handsome fellow around; in fact, he had a goonish look, with a misshapen back and lumpy, clumpy hands. Anyone who watched him, though, soon appreciated him, for he was strong and hard-working. One day the girl Thir the Drudge came along. From the sound of her name alone, you might guess she wasn't pretty, and you'd be right. Her face was pushed in flat, her teeth were stained brown, and her legs were bowed like matching crescent moons. Thraell instantly fell in love with her. They had many ugly sons to whom they gave yucky names, like Kleggi the Horsefly and Fulnir the Stinker. And they had many equally ugly daughters to whom they gave equally yucky names, like Kumba the Stupid and Okkvainkalfa of the Fat Legs. But names and looks aside, these were good people. They worked the land and took care of the animals. From them came the people known as thralls—the people who worked as slaves or servants for all others.

Meanwhile, Heimdall had gone on his way and stopped at a farm. He swung his huge fist against the farmhouse door and then entered. An old couple sat by a fire. They were Afi the Grandpa and Amma

Heimdall visited a poor family, and had a son with the woman Edda. The boy's name was Thraell, and he loved to take care of the animals and plow the fields. His progeny became the servants who worked for other people.

HEIMDALL'S MANY CHILDREN

Heimdall visited another family and had a son with the woman Amma. The boy's name was Karl, and he was good at building huts and barns. His progeny became the free peasants, who did whatever work the servants and slaves didn't do.

the Grandma. On Afi's lap was a piece of wood he was carving into a weaver's beam. Beside Amma was a distaff of flax, from which she spun thread. Their walls were in good repair; their clothes and hair were clean and trim. The old people welcomed Heimdall drily and kept about their work. You know Heimdall, though—he talked about this and that in the most familiar way and soon he was the one sitting closest to the fire and he was the one getting the thickest chunk of rye bread with the biggest glob of butter on it for dinner. After the meal all three went to bed together, with Heimdall in the middle.

Heimdall stayed three nights and three days and then continued his journey. Again, he left behind something: another tiny son, deep inside Amma. When the red-faced babe was born, Amma named him Karl the Free Man. He was stronger than others, and learned skills quickly. He dug the most durable foundations for buildings, erected sturdy huts and barns, and laid thick turfed roofs at just the right pitch. He plowed the land with the help of oxen that he goaded expertly.

When Karl reached manhood, his parents found him a wife called Snor. Keys and little tools, like an awl and a scoop for ear wax, jangled from her waist. Snor used them diligently. She and Karl suited each other, and soon they had a passel of children who were just as neat and diligent as they were and had names to reflect it: One son was Dreng the Strong, another was Smid the Craftsman; one daughter was Brud the Bride, another was Svarri the Proud. From them came the people known as peasants—the people who were free and did most of the work that the thralls didn't do.

Heimdall continued his journey and next met Modir the Mother and Fadir the Father, and you know what happened next: Nine months later Modir gave birth to Jarl the Earl, who was the first in a long line of warriors. In this manner Heimdall gave rise to people of all ranks of society everywhere he went, including the people who became rulers. The kings of Denmark are descended from the god Heimdall himself.

Yes, indeed, Heimdall was important. Majorly.

FREYJA'S SHAME

There was no shortage of beauties among the goddesses, which was good because the deities of this cosmos cared a great deal about looks. A notable beauty was Thor's wife, Sif, the one of the yellow hair that Loki cut off and who now wore an even more amazing golden wig. But more stunning than Sif by far was the magician Freyja. She had come to the Aesir as a kind of peace offering after their war with the Vanir, a tenuous position at best and a lonely one, at least at the start. As fortune had it, she fell in love with Od, and they had two daughters together, Hnoss and Gersemi. So this new life seemed to be working out for her.

Od, however, was a wanderer; one day he simply left Freyja alone. Her hands reached out toward emptiness, her core shook with need. She understood nothing of why he left, where he went. So she wrapped herself well in her cloak of falcon feathers and followed after him. Where? Where? Her tears fell copiously, transforming rock to red-gold puddles wherever she flew.

Life would have been a constant state of mourning if it weren't for Freyja's lovely daughters. They were her treasures. Just gazing at them soothed her. Soon she found all she wanted to do was gaze at beautiful things. She loved gold, especially. Freyja rode in a chariot pulled by two cats or she climbed on the back of her boar, Hildisvini, or she flew in her falcon-feather cloak, always on the lookout for beautiful objects to

PREVIOUS PAGES: Freyja was a Vanir, but she was traded to the Aesir. She loved her Aesir husband, Od. When he disappeared, she searched the cosmos for him, sometimes flying, sometimes on the back of her boar, and sometimes in her chariot pulled by two cats.

The Woes of Beauty

Like Freyja, the women in mythologies around the world often find that trouble comes with beauty. The stunning Aztec goddess Xochiquetzal had a twin sister, Xochipilli, who was kidnapped from her husband and forced to marry another ... and another ... and another. In various voodoo traditions, the spirit of love, Erzulie Fréda Dahomey, is stunning, but angry and disappointed. She wants all men to love her, and that makes her see all women as rivals. The beautiful goddess in a happy marriage is hard to find.

Mural of Xochiquetzal, Palacio Nacional, Mexico City

calm the ache inside that never fully left her.

One night just a little before dawn, Freyja put on her best dress and most elegant brooches. But she didn't call for her chariot or summon her boar or fly in her feathered cloak. Instead, she walked out of Sessrumnir, her hall, and crossed the bridge Bifrost.

Loki happened to be up and about. He jerked to attention as the goddess passed. Where was she going at that hour? Dressed like that? On foot? Here might be an opportunity for making trouble; he followed her.

Winter blanketed Midgard with snow and ice. Now frozen tears dropped with a clink from Freyja's eyes, turning red-gold the grit under her foot. Daylight was brief, but she reached an area of boulders and took a path around them down into a cave. Freyja stood still in the dank air and listened closely.

Freyja went down into the cave that was the smithy of Alfrigg, Dvalinn, Berling, and Grer. She saw the stunning gold necklace they were making and she decided she would have it, no matter what.

Water dripped from the cave ceiling. A little steam rushed over rocks. And there, yes, thud. Thud, thud. The muffled blows of a hammer. That's what she had come for. That's what drove her now to move through the cavern down even deeper into the earth, pulled toward that sound.

The air grew hot, so heavy and hot, the goddess was bathed in sweat. In front of her were four dwarfs pounding away in their smithy—Alfrigg, Dvalinn, Berling, and Grer. They were working on a gold necklace. As Freyja fixed her eyes on it, the metal twisted and writhed like her own heart. It called to her. She needed it.

The four dwarfs for their part gaped at this remarkable goddess. Never had they even dreamed of a vision so alluring.

"Sell me that necklace." Freyja smiled and her teeth lit up the dank smithy. "Name your price."

"It's called Brisingamen," said a dwarf. "And it's not for sale."

You see, the dwarfs, like Loki, didn't fail to recognize an opportunity. They held their faces motionless, their beady eyes unblinking, and they bartered: the necklace in exchange for Freyja taking each of them as her husband for one night. It was a hateful bargain. But Freyja had no husband now, and Brisingamen could bring her solace … joy even. With a dead heart, she made the deal.

Loki waited outside the cave the whole time. Finally Freyja emerged wearing the necklace Brisingamen. Its brilliance nearly blinded the evil one. Loki instantly realized what had happened in those four nights. He lost no time going to Odin, the one-eyed

Loki shape-shifted into a fly and crept through a hole into Freyja's room. As she slept, he turned into Loki again and stole her beautiful necklace.

Allfather, and telling all. Odin knew that Loki was a vile liar, of course. Everyone knew that. Still, the words disturbed him. The gods all noticed Freyja's beauty, no exceptions—not Odin, not even her twin brother, Frey. That those abominable dwarfs should have enjoyed her as their wife made Odin furious with envy. He demanded Loki bring him this dazzling necklace.

Loki went to where Freyja slept in Sessrumnir and found the door locked. Well, that was no problem; he shape-shifted into a fly and flitted around, searching for a hole he could slip through. But the door fit snuggly, top and bottom, the keyhole admitted only a breath, and not a single chink was there between wall plaster and turf. Finally, under the roof, at the very top point of a gable, he found a miniscule hole. He wriggled through.

Freyja slept on her back, the clasp of the necklace under

her neck, out of reach. Loki shape-shifted again, into a flea. He bit her cheek. The goddess groaned and rolled onto her side. Loki shape-shifted into his own form now and unclasped the necklace. He left through the door, identifiable to anyone; there was no longer need to dissemble.

When Freyja woke, her hand went to her throat and met nothing but skin—no gold, no wonderful, fabulous, luxurious gold—gold that had cost her so dearly. It had to be Loki. Who else? And to be that bold, he must have done it under the protection of Odin.

Freyja went straight to Valaskjalf and confronted Odin, sitting on his high seat. "Where is my necklace?"

"You'll never see it again …" Odin waited for Freyja's gasp. Satisfied, he added, "… unless you do as I bid."

His bidding: She was to stir up a war between two human kings in Midgard. And each time a soldier died, she must use magic to make him rise again and fight once more. The battle must go on and on and on. Odin's bidding was hideously bitter; such is the poison of envy.

Freyja swallowed a lump of shame the size of the cosmos. All this for beauty. Beauty was turning out to be Freyja's curse. Her own beauty made men desire her for their wife. Her love of beauty gave men the power to act on that desire. Woe! But even a priestess was helpless against such a powerful enemy.

She held out her hand for that necklace.

THOR'S HAMMER

Thor spent most of his time journeying in his chariot, pulled by his two goats, Tanngrisnir and Tanngnjost, in search of giants to kill. Though he had strength beyond all others, he still relied on three treasures in this quest. One was his belt, Megingjord; it doubled his strength. One was his iron gloves, Jarngreip; when he wore them, he could grip his hammer properly and swing it with effect. And the third was, of course, that hammer, the one that the brother dwarfs Brokk and Sindri had crafted for him: Mjolnir.

One day Thor couldn't find Mjolnir. This was the worst disaster he could imagine: Not only could he not hunt giants without his hammer, he was also vulnerable to whoever had it, as were all the gods. He turned to Loki for help. After all, if you needed a helper who wouldn't be inhibited by scruples, Loki was your man. Besides, Thor actually liked Loki; things were exciting when Loki was around. Together they visited Freyja in Folkvang and asked to borrow her falcon-feather cloak, which she lent willingly, for getting back the hammer was of utmost importance.

Loki flew to the land of the frost giants, directly to their king, Thrym. It was a good guess, for when Loki asked if Thrym had stolen Mjolnir, the massive giant lifted an eyebrow. "The hammer lies eight leagues under the earth. If you want it, bring me Freyja as my bride."

PREVIOUS PAGES: Thor loved nothing more than killing giants. He rode in his chariot pulled by two goats, holding Mjolnir high, ever on the lookout for someone to smash. It's no wonder that the frost giant Thrym stole that hammer.

Loki returned to Thor with the news, and, without a thought to Freyja's welfare, both of them visited the goddess once more and told her to put on a bridal veil, for she was to be wed to Thrym.

Freyja had had her fill of such idiotic demands. "Get out!" she shouted. Her anger made the wonderful necklace Brisingamen burst apart, its jewels scattering across the floor. The walls of her hall, Sessrumnir, rolled like a drum skin.

There was nothing to be done except call together the gods and goddesses to Gladsheim to see if anyone could come up with a less idiotic plan. Heimdall did. "Let's put a bridal veil on Thor."

Everyone guffawed. "We can repair the necklace Brisingamen and Thor can wear it, just as Freyja would." Now the deities howled with laughter. "He can put on a flattering dress with

Powerful Number

Celtic number nine

Nine comes up repeatedly in Norse tales. There are nine worlds; Odin hangs nine days from Yggdrasil and learns nine magical songs; it takes nine days to travel from Midgard to Hel; Heimdall has nine mothers; and Thrym awaits his bride on the ninth night. Nine appears often in tales around the world. Perhaps because human gestation takes nine months? After all, nine is three times three, and a family often begins with one father, one mother, and one baby.

finely crafted silver brooches." Heimdall touched his torso exactly where the brooches would go. "A tangle of keys and tools must hang from his waist …" Heimdall pretended to jangle those keys, "… just as would hang from the waist of any good woman looking to become a good wife." By now a hush had fallen over the hall. Heimdall's plan seemed better with each detail. "And a kerchief over his curly tresses. That should do it."

Thor looked around at all the nodding heads and recoiled. "Do you mean to shame me, making me dress as a woman?"

"Don't be a fool," said Loki. "If Thrym keeps your hammer, giants will rule Asgard. Put on your disguise. I'll travel with you, as your handmaiden, and we'll get back Mjolnir."

So the gods sent word to Thrym that nine nights hence, he'd have his bride.

Thor, dressed as that bride, rode with Loki, dressed as a handmaiden, in the goat-drawn chariot all the way to Jotunheim.

No one said frost giants were particularly smart, but Thrym might have been among the dimmer ones, for he believed Freyja was actually on her way to wed him. He strode about his property making sure everything was in order. His cattle still had gold horns. His oxen were still jet-black. His chests were still brimming with jewels. Everything he had ever wanted was there—except Freyja. And now he'd have her. Life was grand. He ordered a banquet spread on a table and invited everyone who was anyone.

Thor and Loki drove there at such a wild pace that mountains split and the earth caught fire. They swept into Thrym's hall in long dresses, took the seats to the sides of the king's throne, and lost no time chowing down. Thor, disguised as Freyja, devoured an ox and eight salmon. He gobbled down treats that had been prepared for the women guests. He drank crock after crock of mead.

Thrym stared. This woman's appetite excited him. He rubbed his hands together in anticipation. "I've never seen a bride eat or drink like that."

Loki, disguised as the handmaiden, explained that Freyja hadn't eaten for the past eight nights, she was so eager for this wedding.

The frost giant Thrym stole Thor's hammer and wouldn't give it back till Freyja came to marry him. So Thor disguised himself as Freyja and Loki disguised himself as a handmaiden, and they went to Thrym's home for the wedding banquet.

In the middle of the banquet, Thor threw off his disguise and killed Thrym with his hammer, Mjolnir. Then he killed the other frost giants who had come as wedding guests.

Thrym grinned in his stupidity. It didn't seem right to make such a lusty wife wait for a kiss. He lifted her veil, and then leaped back with a gasp. "Her eyes are sizzling coals!"

Again Loki rose to the occasion. He explained that Freyja hadn't slept for the past eight nights, she was so eager for this wedding.

At this moment Thrym's older sister offered the bride her loyalty in exchange for the rings on her fingers and on her handmaiden's fingers.

Thrym paid no attention to this hag of a sister, as well he shouldn't have. Who knew what was up with her? Perhaps the whole family was a bunch of dolts. Instead, he merrily called for the hammer Mjolnir, which he somehow saw as intrinsic to this wedding. He had the hammer placed on his bride's lap, near those warm thighs. The next moment Thor grabbed his hammer, ripped off his veil, and glared at everyone. His eyes and beard flamed. With one blow of Mjolnir, he smashed Thrym's skull. Then he smashed the skull of every giant guest at the wedding feast, including Thrym's luckless old sister.

It was Thrym who had stolen the hammer in the first place, not his sister and not his guests. Yet all of them lay slaughtered. Humans loved Thor; they saw him as protecting them against the giants. But was he protecting anyone that night?

Thor worried that dressing as a woman would shame him. No, no, no. His own taste for blood and gore—that was the real dishonor in him. Shame, shame on Thor.

THOR THE GREEDY

The more Thor thought about giants, the more he wanted to kill them. He was obsessed. So one morning he said he'd head east on a killing spree, and when Loki offered to tag along, Thor agreed. Theirs was a twisted alliance.

They set out in the goat-drawn chariot and spent the full day traveling across Midgard. Come evening, they stopped at a humble farm and asked for room and board. The farmer's wife offered these weary guests room quite readily, but she apologized that the board could only be vegetable gruel, for there was but little meat.

Thor said he'd supply the meat, and he swiftly slaughtered his two goats. He set the skin aside and told the farmer's family to throw the dinner bones on the skins as they ate. The hungry farmer gaped at such a feast. But after the meat was gone, the farmer's son Thjalfi stared at a goat thighbone. Marrow was far too delicious and nutritious to waste. He snuck over and split that bone, sucked out the marrow, and tossed it onto the bone pile.

That night all slept soundly.

In the morning Thor woke first. He held the hammer Mjolnir over the bone-filled goat skins and muttered magic words. Instantly, the goats were whole again, and fully alive. But one had a lame hind leg. Thor stomped into the room where the farm family slept still. "Who broke my goat's

PREVIOUS PAGES:
Thor and Loki went hunting giants. They stopped at a peasant home and ate heartily, offering their own goats as meat—magic goats that would come alive again later. But the peasants' son cracked a goat bone—a mistake with terrible consequences.

The Norse Diet

In the last story Thor devoured an ox, eight salmon, and other treats, and later in this chapter we'll see an extravagant eating contest. The idea that gods might eat huge amounts must have been appealing to the Norse people because the harsh, long winters meant farmers spent much time simply trying to get enough food for their families. They grew vegetables and grains and collected fruits. The Norse also hunted game, raised animals, and fished. They ate this fish fresh, smoked, salted, or fermented.

Hanging fish to dry is an old Viking tradition.

thighbone?" He raised Mjolnir high in threat.

The farmer offered anything, anything at all, if he would spare their lives.

Now, Thor was quick to anger, obviously, but also quick to regain his senses. The terrified faces of the family gave him pause. With a wave of the hand he said he'd simply take the boy Thjalfi and his sister Roskva as his servants, and that would be that.

The idea of balance—of a punishment that fit the crime— was foreign to Thor. That these two children should hereafter spend their lives in servitude never fazed him, such was his sense of self-importance. But then, he was a god—and gods were important, after all.

So Thor and Loki and the boy Thjalfi and his sister Roskva set out on foot till they reached the seashore. They slept on an open strand. In the morning they found an old boat and crossed the waters into Utgard, which surrounded the stronghold of the giants in Jotunheim. Then Thjalfi ran ahead, scouting, and found an enormous hall in a pine glade for them to sleep in. In the middle of the night, however, they woke to a great trembling underfoot—the whole earth roared. Thor was sure it was an earthquake, but no sooner than he said that, it stopped. Still, they didn't feel safe staying where they were. So they explored the grand hall and found a side room, where three of them entered; Thor stood guard at the doorway with Mjolnir at the ready. But no one slept really; how could they with the roaring returning intermittently as it did? Dread sat like mud in their mouths.

In the morning Thor crept outside and saw a giant asleep. This was a bigger giant than any Thor had ever known before. The giant snored. Aha! the source of the roars. As Thor stood there, the giant woke. Thor was so surprised, he didn't kill him, but, instead, acted sensible and asked who he was.

"Skrymir," said the giant. And he asked if Thor and his crew had moved his glove.

Instantly Thor understood. The enormous hall they'd slept in was Skrymir's glove, and the side room was the thumb part. Amazing!

Skrymir offered to share food. Then he accompanied them on their journey. But his strides were so long and so fast that the others were soon left behind and didn't catch up to him

till nightfall, when he had stopped to sleep. Again, he let them raid his knapsack for food, but he fell asleep as they did so. Thor and Loki and Thjalfi and Roskva wrestled with the knot on that sack, but they couldn't open it. Thor became convinced that this was exactly what Skrymir had intended. In his too typical fury, he slammed the giant on the forehead with Mjolnir. The hammer broke the skin.

The giant woke. "What leaf fell on my head?"

Yikes. Mjolnir had barely wounded the giant, much less killed him. The four snuck away and worried half the night. But Skrymir's snoring irritated Thor so much that he went

Thor was annoyed at the noisy snoring of the giant Skrymir; he climbed onto the sleeping giant's head and slammed him with his hammer. But the giant was so enormous, all he did was wake up surprised.

THOR THE GREEDY

back and slammed Mjolnir with all his might against the giant's forehead.

The giant woke. "Did an acorn fall on my head?"

Yikes and double yikes. But this giant didn't seem threatening, not really. So, near dawn Thor tiptoed back and swung Mjolnir harder than ever into the giant's temple.

The giant woke. "Bird droppings—they must have fallen on me." Now he saw Thor. "Gather your party and go home. The folk ahead are much larger than me." Then Skrymir took his sack and marched north into the mountains.

But Thor and his companions persisted through the forest until they came to a high gate. They forced their way between the bars and entered a huge hall, where giants lolled on benches and leered at them. The giant king said he knew this puny thing before him was the god Thor, and he challenged the travelers to display a skill.

Loki took the challenge. "I can eat faster than anyone."

A giant named Logi sat at the opposite of a wooden trencher from him. Servants filled it with food. Then Loki and Logi ate their way toward each other. But Logi the giant ate not only the food but the bones and trencher as well. He won.

"Who's next?" asked the giant king.

Thjalfi said, "I can run faster than anyone."

A small guy named Hugi—a giant, but small for a giant—raced Thjalfi. Hugi easily won. They raced three

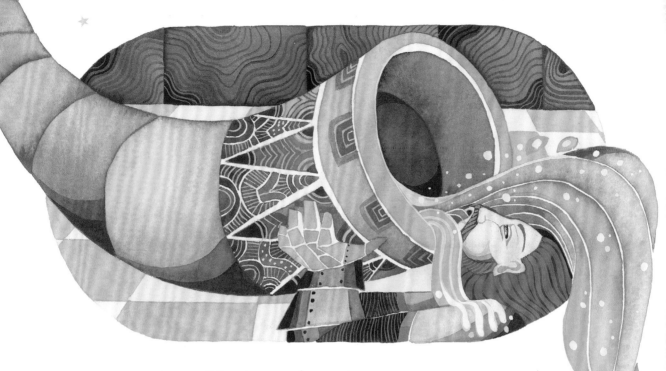

Thor bet a giant king that he could drink more than anyone. The giant gave him a full horn. Thor drank and drank, but he couldn't drain the horn.

times. Hugi won three times.

"And you, Thor?" asked the giant king.

"I can drink more than anyone," said Thor.

"Quite a boast," said the giant king. He gave Thor a horn to drain.

Thor took an enormous draught. But much still remained in the horn. He took a second draught. And a third. It was as though the horn held a rising tide.

"Bah! Give me a second task," said Thor. "Anything."

"Boast away, will you?" The giant king challenged Thor to pick up his cat.

Thor tugged on the cat, but its paws stayed on the ground even as its back stretched and arched higher and higher. Thor pushed himself under the cat and heaved himself upward. The most that moved was a single paw.

"Bah!" Thor screamed. "I want a third challenge. Someone wrestle with me!"

The giants laughed. Only the old giantess Elli hobbled forward; she dropped her walking stick. It was shameful to fight a woman, but Thor was eager to clear his name. He lunged at her. She stood firm. He persisted. She brought him to his knees.

"Enough," said the giant king. "Let's feast and then rest."

And so all ate and drank themselves silly and slept in the huge hall, and the giant king showed a generosity that Thor couldn't fathom.

The next day Thor and his companions left. The giant king accompanied them out to the forest. Thor was

After failing at two tasks, Thor asked for someone to wrestle him, for he thought he could beat anyone. But an old giantess named Elli defeated him.

chagrined that he had failed, and feared the giant king would bad-mouth him to everyone. But the giant king explained that he had cast a spell on them. All that had happened was partly illusion. The giant king was, in fact, that giant Skrymir, and if Thor's hammer had hit its mark, it would have killed him. The giant Logi, who won the eating contest against Loki and consumed even the trencher, was really wildfire. The giant Hugi, who won the race against Thjalfi, was really the giant king's thoughts. The horn that Thor couldn't drain had its bottom in the sea. The cat he couldn't lift was the serpent Jormungand, who circled Midgard and bit his own tail. And Elli was old age itself. So Thor and his companions had, in fact, done very well in these challenges and proven themselves worthy. "But don't come back," said the giant king. "I used magic to vanquish you this time. I'll use it again. I'll protect Utgard however I must."

Amazing! This giant was far better at deception than even Loki! In anger at having been tricked, Thor raised his hammer. But the giant king had already vanished. Thor chased after him, ready to crush the huge hall with Mjolnir, but the hall had also vanished.

Thor went back home, stopping by the farm to get his two goats, but keeping Thjalfi and Roskva as servants. He was a greedy god; mercy meant nothing to him.

IDUNN'S APPLES

No one was guaranteed eternal life to their bodies. Death could claim anyone. But the gods, at least—unlike the humans, the giants, and the dwarfs—could go on living with youthful vitality unless something came along to cut them down. How the gods managed not to age and wither was no secret; it was because of the goddess Idunn.

Idunn had apples. And they were not ordinary. Anyone who had a bite became rejuvenated. How Idunn came to own those apples nobody knew, but she was a magician, for sure, and she fed her apples to the gods, and no one else. Everyone in the cosmos knew about Idunn and those apples.

Now one summer morning, Odin, Loki, and Hoenir went exploring a part of Midgard that was new to them. Odin was his usual bold self; Loki was his usual cunning self; and Hoenir—well, he was his usual taciturn self. Remember, he was the Aesir god, brother of Odin, who had been sent to live among the Vanir after the war between the two tribes of gods. It was Hoenir who made good judgments for the Vanir, but only with Mimir's help. On his own, he kept his mouth shut.

The three gods tramped all day long. They followed a pebble-ridden glacier stream down into a valley and came across a herd of oxen—lucky for them, since they were famished. Loki killed an ox and Odin and Hoenir built a fire to roast it. The aroma was mouthwatering.

PREVIOUS PAGES: A huge eagle ate the gods' meal. When Loki speared him, he found his hand was magically stuck to the weapon. In exchange for his freedom, Loki promised the eagle what he demanded: Idunn and her precious apples.

But somehow the meat simply wasn't getting cooked.

Wise Odin guessed the problem. "Someone's working against us."

"Me," came the screech from an oak branch above them. The gods looked up at an enormous eagle. "Let me eat first. Then what's left will cook to perfection for you."

Since they had no choice, the gods agreed.

The eagle swooped down and set to eating a shoulder. Then a second. Then half the rump. Then the other half. What would be left? In a fury, Loki rammed his staff through the bird.

The bird screeched again and flew off, with the staff still piercing it and with Loki hanging on, for the god found that his hand was stuck to the staff. The eagle flew low to the ground and Loki banged along. Rocks and

Nourishing Apples

The apple tree originated in central Asia and may have been the first tree to be cultivated. Apples have been grown in Asia and Europe for thousands of years. They were brought to North America by European colonists in the 17th century. The old saying

"An apple a day keeps the doctor away" turns out to be right: Apples and apple products are important to child nutrition. So the appearance of apples in these old Norse tales, and their association to continued strength and vitality, is no surprise.

Apples play a part in myths from many cultures.

thorns scratched his legs and feet till they bled.

"Mercy!" called Loki.

The eagle flew close beside a glacier till Loki bled everywhere.

"Mercy!" cried Loki.

"Only if you swear ..."

"What? I'll swear to anything!"

"... to bring me Idunn and her apples." The eagle smashed Loki against boulders now.

"I swear!"

"One week," screeched the eagle. And he dropped Loki like a sack of broken bones.

The next week, as Idunn walked along with her basket full of golden apples, Loki ran up to her. "You won't believe what I've seen," he said.

And well she shouldn't have, for Loki was about to lie, as usual. But Idunn paused and listened.

"A tree with golden apples that look just like yours," said Loki. "Maybe they, too, are magical. The tree's in the forest, on the other side of the bridge Bifrost. Come with me. Bring your apples to compare, and if those other apples really are the same, we'll gather them for the gods."

So Idunn crossed Bifrost with Loki. The instant she stepped off the flaming bridge, the eagle swooped down and carried Idunn and her basket of apples away, over the sea, straight to Jotunheim.

Loki met Idunn as she walked along holding her basket full of the golden apples that the gods nibbled on. Those apples kept the gods young and strong. He convinced her to cross Bifrost with him.

Loki wasn't surprised at all. Jotunheim was the land of the giants, and Loki was already convinced that the eagle was in truth a giant. He was right: It was the giant Thjazi, who now locked Idunn in his home high in the mountains.

Soon enough the gods noticed Idunn's absence. The alarming consequences made them shudder. They grew thin and weak. Their bones became birdlike. Their skin fell in soft folds. The eyes of some turned milky, their sight dim. The hands of some trembled. That one over there went bald.

That one turned yellow with constipation, and that other one, red with the runs. They were tired, irritable, fragile. Now some spoke nonsense, while others couldn't find the words they'd always known, and others had no voice even if the words danced in their head. Old age was no picnic.

Odin drew on what little energy remained within him and called a meeting in the hall Gladsheim. Everyone came except Idunn and Loki.

It didn't take much to put two and two together and realize that Loki had stayed away because all of this was his fault. They had to find the trickster and force him to tell them where Idunn had gone.

The decrepit gods shuffled along till they found Loki asleep in a field. They bound him and dragged him back

While Idunn was locked in the home of the giant Thjazi, the gods suffered without her apples. They grew old and weak.

to Odin. Weakened and helpless, Loki told all. He'd had no choice; the eagle, who was really the giant Thjazi, would have killed him if he hadn't promised to bring him Idunn and her apples.

"Yes, you had to promise. But did you have to keep your promise?" asked Odin. It was a good question. For a liar like Loki, not keeping the promise should have been natural. So he'd kept that promise just to cause all this misery among the gods. "We'll split your ribs," said Odin. "They'll spread like wings—like those of the eagle you befriended."

"No!" screamed Loki. "I'll bring back Idunn and her apples, if Freyja will lend me her falcon-feather cloak."

Freyja handed the cloak to Loki, and wiped the few remaining fallen hairs from her shoulders. She was now

IDUNN'S APPLES

completely bald, ravaged by old age.

"You're not so beautiful anymore," said Loki.

Freyja just wept those red-gold tears.

Enclosed in the feather cloak, Loki became a falcon. He flew to Thrymheim, high in the mountains of Jotunheim.

There Idunn huddled in a drafty room, waiting in fear for Thjazi to return from wherever he had gone. Loki turned Idunn into a nut and carried her in his claws back toward Asgard. Meanwhile, Thjazi came home with his daughter Skadi, saw that Idunn was missing, shape-shifted into an eagle, and flew after her. He was stronger than Loki—he gained on that falcon.

But Odin saw it all from his high seat, Hlidskjalf. He had all the gods gather wood shavings and set an enormous fire. Those teetering gods shook as they picked up a piece of kindling here, another there, but they did it. The fire was tremendous. Loki flew over it, but by the time Thjazi reached there, the flames were so high, they burned him up.

Loki chanted magic words to the nut.

Idunn stood among them again, young and fresh, and holding out apples.

SKADI & NJORD

High in Thrymheim, Skadi watched her father, the giant Thjazi, shape-shift into an eagle and chase after Loki. An eagle is stronger than a falcon. And Thjazi was accustomed to flying as a bird, while Loki was new to it. Thjazi would catch the wily Loki and bring back Idunn and her apples, and Skadi and her father would be forever young.

All Skadi had to do was wait. But she wasn't good at waiting. So she wandered the mountain. The scree moved underfoot with a crunch, crunch, as broken rock does. The brightness of the sheets of snow made her squint. The damp seeped through her skin and deep into her bones. What a dreary wasteland this part of Jotunheim was. Skadi smiled. It made her giantess heart throb with love. Nothing was better than sharing a bleak day in Thrymheim with her father.

Only something was wrong. The hours passed, the night grew old, and still Thjazi didn't come back. Skadi picked at her elbows, at her knees, at the bumps on her toes, as she imagined the gods of Asgard playing some rotten trick on Thjazi. They were a bloody bunch; nothing was beneath them. By the time dawn came, a rocklike certainty had lodged in her stomach: Her father was dead.

Skadi put on a coat of chain mail. She put on a helmet. She touched each red beak and looked into all the shining eyes of the bird heads inlaid on the hide of her father's tough

PREVIOUS PAGES:
Skadi, the giantess daughter of Thjazi, figured out that her missing father must have been slayed. Here she wears a helmet and coat of mail and carries her father's shield and spear. She is ready for revenge against the Aesir.

Winter Travel

Skadi zoomed across snow on skis; that's how she hunted. The ski goes back in history farther than the wheel, perhaps more than 20,000 years. A cave drawing in Lyon, France, from Paleolithic times suggests that Cro-Magnon man hunted reindeer during the last ice age on snowshoes, skis, and sleds. Skiing spread from Europe to Asia and then into North America. After many years, the entire Northern Hemisphere used skis. Our word "ski" comes from the Old Norse *ski*, stick.

Skiing is an important part of Norse culture.

shield. She closed her fingers tight around the white ash shaft of his battle spear.

Finally, she hung at her hip her father's sword. The giant Surt had a flaming sword that he would swing against the Aesir at the terrible final battle, Ragnarok. The god Heimdall had the sword Hofud that knew everything in his head and thus slashed with intelligence. The god Frey had a sword that fought all on its own. But Skadi's father's sword was even better. It was incised with a serpent that struck terror into an enemy heart just as surely as venom.

Well armed, Skadi headed for Asgard, her lips puckered for the sweet kiss of vengeance.

Heimdall saw her coming, of course; he did his job of guard well. He blew Gjallarhorn to call the gods together.

When Skadi arrived at the foot of the bridge Bifrost, the gods had already assembled. They had no wish to see more bloodshed, so they offered Skadi gold in recompense for her father's death.

Skadi shrugged. What good could gold do her? She owned a mountain of gold. But she looked across at those gods and noticed that some of them weren't hard on the eyes. One, in fact, was like eye candy—a certain Balder (for this was before the fair Balder had been slain). Skadi was a hot-blooded giantess. Yes, she grieved for her father's companionship. But that Balder—ooh— he would sure add a spark to the dank nights in Thrymheim. So she said, instead of making off with a sack of gold, she'd pick a husband. "Gentle. Wise. And I won't leave until I've had a bellyful of laughter."

Now Skadi was not bad-looking herself. And the gods had often taken giantesses as wives. So Skadi's demand was not unthinkable. Still, Odin couldn't help but see that Skadi's eye had rested a little too long on Balder, and Balder was his favorite—it wouldn't do to let Skadi make decisions that affected Balder's life. So Odin agreed. "On one condition," he said. "You must choose your husband by his feet. All the rest of him will be covered."

That didn't sound off to Skadi. After all, a man as meltingly gorgeous as Balder surely had

The giantess Skadi wanted revenge for the death of her father, Thjazi. So Odin let her choose a husband as her repayment— but she had to choose him by looking only at his feet.

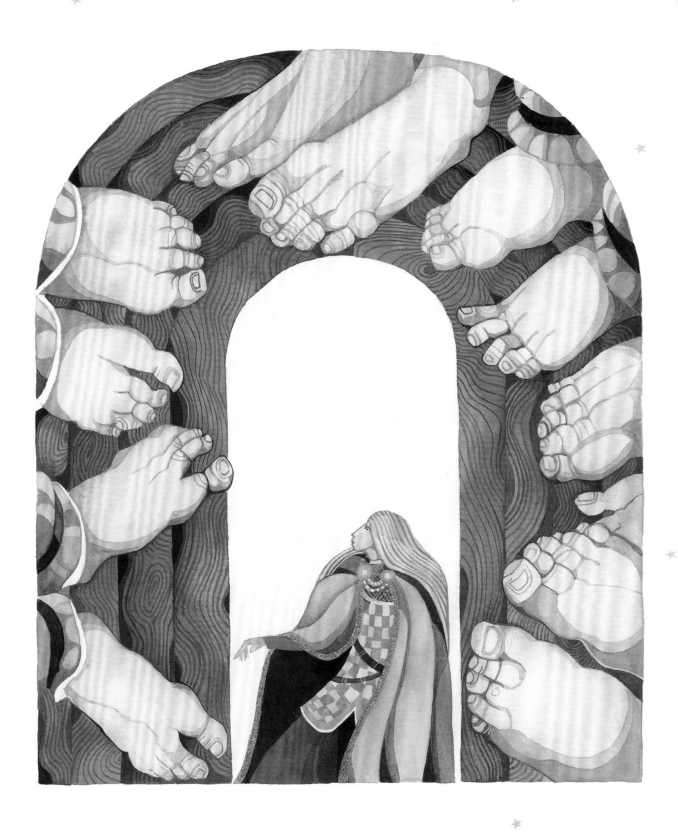

caressable feet. So the gods covered themselves but for their feet, and Skadi chose easily.

Only it turned out she had chosen Njord. Njord was a rather rough-and-tumble god. He was one of the Vanir originally and had been traded after the war, so now he lived among the Aesir with his son Frey and his daughter Freyja. He was the god of seafaring folk and he looked the part: weathered cheeks, sea blue eyes, sea salt in his hair. He wasn't what Skadi wanted. No, not at all.

But before Skadi could protest, Njord held up a warning hand. "Harsh words have no place at the beginning of a marriage."

"I've been tricked," said Skadi.

"Better me than Loki, no?" answered Njord.

Odin nodded. "Gentle and wise. You've got your husband, Skadi."

The giantess Skadi demanded that she be made to laugh before she would agree to marry Njord. So Loki told a joke so funny that Skadi couldn't keep herself from laughing.

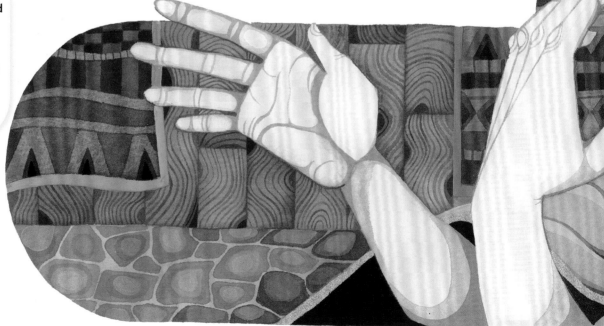

"But the bellyful of laughter? Where is that?" Skadi shook her head. "I'll never laugh again."

So Loki took over. The trickster liked to think of himself as a problem solver, after all. He told a bawdy story about a goat accompanying him to market and a tug-of-war that involved a lot of noise and no small amount of pain to Loki's private parts, and in the confusion of telling it all, he fell back into Skadi's arms. The giantess laughed in spite of herself.

And so Skadi had all that she had required. There was no way she could back out of the bargain now.

But Odin decided to sweeten the deal further. He took from his pouch two wet marbles. Skadi gasped as the eyes of her father stared at her. Odin flung them high so they clung to the sky, twin stars to gleam down on Skadi.

Njord held out his hand, inviting his new wife to come live with him at his beloved shipyard, Noatun. Then began the first struggle of many between the newlyweds, for Skadi said she'd never live anywhere but Thrymheim. At last they agreed to spend nine nights in one home and then nine nights in the other. They began with Thrymheim, for Njord had a gentlemanly streak. But the god soon learned he hated those frozen

The god Njord loved his ship-yard, and the giantess Skadi loved her snowy mountains. Though they were husband and wife, they couldn't find any place to live that made them both happy.

mountains; they felt like death to him. The howling of the wolves kept him awake. After nine nights they went to Noatun. But the giantess soon learned she hated the sight of the boats rocking on the sea endlessly, endlessly. Worse was the whooping of the swans and the mewing of the gulls. She got no sleep, not even when Njord sang stories to her.

It wasn't long before husband and wife parted, each to live in their own realm. Njord heard about Skadi often, and every now and then he saw her—a fleet figure skiing across the snowscapes, determined in her desolation.

Some marriages just aren't meant to be.

FREY & GERD

Frey was Njord's son. He was a Vanir by origin, but when his father was traded to the Aesir after the great war, he and his sister Freyja accompanied the old man. That was fine with Frey; the gods were good to him. As a babe, when he cut his first tooth, the gods held the usual teething celebration and gave him rule over all Alfheim as a gift. The light elves of that land loved him, and why not? Frey was god of sunshine and sweet breezes. He rode around in a wagon pulled by the boar Gullinbursti, whose gold mane lit the way, and he strewed flowers and fruits to onlookers. Or he sailed in his ship Skidbladnir, the ship that always found winds to drive it in the direction the captain wished. Humans loved this god, too, for he brought the season when plants grew. He was responsible for the fertility of the cosmos. The only ones who didn't love Frey, in fact, were the giants. They had little tolerance for sunshine and sweet breezes, after all. They liked Jotunheim icy. And Frey returned their hostility with his own. Frost giants were a scourge upon the cosmos as far as he was concerned.

So, while Frey lived in Alfheim, he felt entirely at home in Asgard. In fact, he felt so at home that one day he did something he had no right to do, something only Odin and his goddess wife, Frigg, did: He sat on the high seat Hlidskjalf and looked out over the nine worlds. That's when his troubles began.

PREVIOUS PAGES:
Frey did the unthinkable: He sat on Odin's throne. From there, he saw the gorgeous young giantess Gerd. The sun shone down on her and made her sparkle. Frey fell instantly in love—a desperate situation for him, since he had always hated giants.

He looked north toward Jotunheim. One of the biggest halls there belonged to the giant Gymir. And Gymir had a daughter. A lovely daughter. Oh, what a smashingly lovely daughter. This daughter, glorious Gerd, came out of her father's fine hall just as Frey was looking her way. As she turned to shut the hall doors behind her, the light of all nine worlds glistened on her arms. She sparkled brighter than gold, brighter than stars, brighter even than sun on snow.

Frey stared. He couldn't take his eyes off Gerd.

When the girl closed herself inside her own hall, Frey finally shut his eyes. But the image of her burned in his brain. He could see nothing else. He stumbled from Odin's hall aching with longing. He couldn't sleep. He couldn't eat. He pined for Gerd. Frey was lovesick—afflicted.

Midnight Sun

Aurora borealis in Norway

All the lands north of the Arctic Circle have long days in summer—so much so that on some days the sun shines continually—and short days in winter—so much so that on some days the sun never shines. For Norway the darkness of winter is combined with steep mountains and deep, cold fjords. Winds can make it nearly impossible to walk outside. All these facts make winter exceptionally lonely for people who do not live with others. So when Skirnir threatens Gerd in this story with never having a husband, he is relying on her fear of torturous isolation.

Now Njord had plenty of problems of his own, what with a wife who wouldn't live with him, but his son's behavior worried him. So he sent Frey's servant Skirnir to find out what was wrong.

Frey told Skirnir of his love, and of his fear that marriage between the two would never be approved of because the giants held no love for any Aesir, especially not their enemy Frey. Still, overwhelmed by his passion, he bade Skirnir fetch the girl.

But Skirnir needed help. He asked Frey to lend him his magic sword that could fight on its own, protecting whomever wielded it. And he asked for Frey's horse that could find its way through the dark and wasn't hurt by flames. Frey gave these treasures … ultimately a foolish decision, but a god in love is as much a fool as anyone.

Skirnir rode that horse as hard as he could. He convinced the ferryman to take them across the river into Jotunheim. By now it was the pitch of night, but that horse galloped on—for he could find his way through the dark. Then they came to a curtain of fire, but that horse galloped on—for he wasn't hurt by flames. The next morning they arrived at last.

Fierce dogs guarded Gerd's hall. They barked and growled. When Gerd heard the commotion, she told her servant to welcome the visitor, though her mouth went sour and her ears buzzed eerily.

And so Skirnir was brought before Gerd, who was dressed all

in white. He offered her 11 apples from Idunn's tree to marry Frey. "Think of your beauty lasting and lasting."

But not even the promise of everlasting youth could persuade Gerd to marry the giants' lethal enemy.

Skirnir held out the ring Draupnir that the dwarf Brokk had given to Odin. How it came to be in Skirnir's hands was anyone's guess. "This ring drops eight others just as beautiful every ninth night."

But who needed wealth? Gerd's father, Gymir, had a hall full of jewels.

Playing the nice guy was getting Skirnir nowhere; Skirnir unsheathed Frey's sword. "Your choice: beheading or marriage?"

But Gerd said her father would fight Frey and win.

Frey fell in love with the beautiful giantess, Gerd. He sent his servant, Skirnir, to fetch her. Skirnir offered her 11 of Idunn's apples if she'd marry Frey. But the promise of eternal youth wasn't enough to convince her.

Skirnir now raised his own staff, which had magic untold. Gerd gaped at it, spellbound, as Skirnir spoke. "If you don't marry Frey, you will never marry anyone. You will sit alone in your hall, bleak, feeling nothing against your skin ever but sleet and cutting wind. You will fly into unaccountable rages and you will weep for days on end. You will crawl like the lowliest of creatures through the halls of the frost giants, having no sense of why you do it and no ability to stop yourself. You will scream with the need of a husband, and never, never

Skirnir got furious at Gerd for refusing to marry Frey. He threatened her with loneliness for all the rest of time. His words scared her. But they didn't convince her. It was his magic staff that finally made her love Frey, not any promises or threats.

attract anyone to your side. Everything you drink will taste like waste, but you'll drink it all the same, for you'll never slake your thirst. It's your choice, Gerd. No joy, all pain—or a marriage to Frey."

Gerd listened closely through the venomous words. She trembled. The threat meant she would lose everything she valued in her womanhood; she would never attract a husband, never have children. Her fertility would be forever thwarted. Still, she was firm in her refusal.

Until she looked up at that magic staff. It loomed above her. She couldn't take her eyes off it. Now she spoke slowly. She said, "I never would have believed that I could love a god." Skirnir's offers of presents hadn't worked. Skirnir's threats of violence hadn't worked. But simply by looking at that magic staff, somehow Gerd had changed. She loved Frey. Why? How? But the answers didn't matter. She loved him. And so she promised to be his wife nine days hence.

When Skirnir came back with the good news, Frey thought he couldn't survive the wait of nine days. But he did, of course, wed the maid.

What he didn't realize was that he couldn't survive the loss of his magic sword, for Skirnir didn't bring it back from Jotunheim. That sword would have been useful to Frey in the final battle, Ragnarok. Perhaps he could have won against the fire giant Surt instead of dying hideously. Perhaps if he had wooed Gerd himself rather than letting Skirnir steal her through dishonorable means, he might have won the girl and kept his sword.

But perhaps not. Fate is fate, after all. And given what he did to Gerd, maybe Frey got the end he deserved.

DEATH BY BLUNDER

DEATH BY BLUNDER

Frigg was Odin's wife, and she took her role as head goddess seriously. As she saw it, it wasn't a husband that a wife needed to attend to. Her own husband was headstrong and bullish and, well, she couldn't really influence him much even if she tried. Odin was convinced that women were fickle creatures, and simple-minded, as well. The fairer his words were to Frigg, the more she knew his thoughts were false. He trusted no one, which made him untrustworthy himself. So Frigg didn't waste energy and time on Odin. Instead, she focused on what a woman could do that a man couldn't—childbearing. Frigg helped all women in childbirth. She bid laboring women to lie on a bed of grasses that had yellow flowers whose pungent scent quickly killed the fleas that ran up and down their bodies. The women relaxed into a half swoon; birth was far more palatable this way, especially because of Frigg's voice: She spoke to them of motherly love. She became goddess of love, but not the romantic stimulation that Freyja evoked, rather the all-encompassing devotion that one has for another throughout life. Frigg knew everything there was to know about that kind of love, for that's how she loved her children, the gods Balder and Hod. She adored them. She raised them in her hall, Fensalir, and showered them with kisses.

Perhaps that's why these gods were so unique. Hod was completely blind and tremendously strong. He held back

PREVIOUS PAGES: Frigg, Odin's wife, adored her two sons. Hod, known for being blind, was always willing to help. Balder, known for being handsome, was peaceful. Both were sweet-tempered, perhaps because they were loved so much.

Frigg's Grass

Bedstraw, *Galium verum*

Galium verum, commonly known as yellow bedstraw, grows throughout Europe and Asia. In medieval times it was used to stuff mattresses, since its odor kills fleas. Its yellow flowers were used to coagulate milk in making cheese. Its roots made red dye; its flowers, yellow. Its leaves made a mild sedative. And in Denmark it is used even today in the alcoholic drink *bjæsk*. Perhaps this was Frigg's grass that she used to help birthing mothers with—Frigg, the saddest mother ever.

from the others, always listening, ready to oblige. He became god of the darkness that settled in winter, and that was fine with him. Winter was long and powerful, and quiet, like him. And winter always came back—in the end, winter prevailed. Like motherly love.

Balder was almost the opposite of Hod; he was light and airy. And unlike most other Aesir gods, he didn't shout or stomp around. He didn't go violent at the slightest provocation. He was thoughtful, gentle. Ultimately, he was wise, but in a different way from his father, Odin. Instead of knowing all and understanding every fact with his intellect, he intuited the cosmos. He empathized with every living thing and then beyond, with every tree and rock, with every breeze and grain of sand and droplet of dew. Balder was an anomaly in that

cosmos; without any inkling of the treachery of others, he was doomed—a bird without wings.

So when Balder reported having bad dreams to his mother, when he said he woke from dreams about ghostly skulls with the stench of his own death in his mouth, Frigg wasn't surprised. Her son was too pure for this reality, this cosmos. Besides, she'd been waiting for this moment. Like Odin she saw much of the future—imperfectly, to be sure—but definitely. She didn't speak of it. What was the point of telling others about things they couldn't change? The anticipation would only make them suffer and, probably, reduce them to ditherers, for helplessness undoes a soul. So, no, she didn't blink twice at Balder's news.

But Frigg was the head goddess. She was Queen of Asgard. She was the only one besides Odin who was allowed to climb up onto the high seat Hlidskjalf and view the

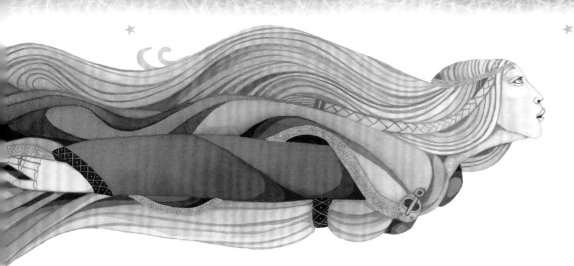

entire cosmos. Frigg was not about to stand by and do nothing. Dread had sharpened her teeth and eyes and fingertips.

Oh, she held her tongue for a while, to allow Odin time to do his thing. Odin was Allfather, after all. He needed to assume control. Odin called an assembly to discuss the possible portents of Balder's nightmares. Then he rode his eight-legged steed, Sleipnir, down to Niflheim and conferred there with a prophetess, a certain sibyl, who told him everything that would come to pass. It was all for nothing, of course, because Odin already knew the future. But as a father, he must have hoped against hope that he was wrong for once. He must have ground his teeth down to the pulp, gnashing out that hope. He came back and shook his shaggy head sadly at Frigg.

So Frigg was now free to go into action. She flew through the cosmos, for she had a flying cloak just as Freyja did, and extracted a promise from fire, water, metals, stones, trees, diseases, beasts, birds, poisons, and serpents that they would do Balder no harm. No one, nothing refused her request. And thus Balder seemed invulnerable.

But to test that, someone threw a pebble at him. Balder didn't

Balder had nightmares that he would die. So his mother, Frigg, wife of Odin, flew through the cosmos, exacting promises from everything she passed that they would do Balder no harm.

feel it. Someone else threw a stick. No reaction. Ha! The gods found this turn of events delightful. It soon became good sport to stab Balder or, at the very least, cast stones at him, only to see the handsome god stand there unhurt and smiling.

Loki hated this. Balder was getting all the attention. So he disguised himself as an old woman and visited Frigg. He complained about the poor man who was being stoned, as though he didn't know the whole story of Balder's invulnerability. When Frigg explained that man was her son and this was no stoning, this was just sport that could come to no bad end because of the cosmos' promise, the disguised Loki asked if by chance there was any element that had not sworn to do Balder no harm. Frigg should have been on the alert. She should have suspected an ulterior motive, even from this unimposing and doddering woman. But somehow, she didn't. She answered forthrightly: One little mistletoe was too young for Frigg to ask a favor of.

Loki pulled up that mistletoe and made darts from it.

Then the trickster pulled the worst trick of his life, the worst trick of the cosmos. He got Hod to join in the game of throwing things at Balder—something Hod had never done before; it made no sense for a blind one to throw things. But Loki guided Hod's hand. And, of course, in that hand he put the

Hod was the blind brother of Balder. Loki tricked him into throwing a mistletoe dart at Balder—and Loki guided blind Hod's hand. The dart killed poor Balder.

DEATH BY BLUNDER

mistletoe darts. Hod threw; alas, he unwittingly killed his own dear brother. The whole of Asgard was bereft. Frigg asked who would dare go down to Hel and offer her a ransom to let Balder come back. Another of Odin's sons, Hermod, volunteered. He mounted Odin's steed Sleipnir and traveled nine nights down into the realm of Hel to beg Balder's release, for the whole cosmos loved him.

Hel said that so long as the whole cosmos wept for Balder, she would let him free. But if anyone refused to weep, Balder would belong to Hel till the final battle.

So now the Aesir sent messengers throughout the cosmos asking everyone to weep Balder out of Hel. And everyone did. Everyone except the giantess Thokk, who some say was Loki in disguise. That was enough to seal Balder's fate.

Odin looked around for revenge. Frigg couldn't meet his eyes—Hod was her son, too, after all. She stayed hidden behind her curtain of tears. So Odin took the giantess Rindr as his wife and that very day she gave birth to the god Vali,

> Hel agreed that if everyone in the cosmos cried for Balder, she would set him free. And everyone did—they wailed in misery— everyone except the giantess Thokk. That was enough to ruin it; Balder could not escape Hel.

who grew to adulthood before the night fell and slew the hapless Hod. Now there were 12 major gods, but, alas, two of them were doomed to Hel.

And so Balder stayed in Hel, awaiting the battle Ragnarok, when he'd be set free, alongside his brother Hod, whose head lay heavy in his own hands. And Odin dreamed of Balder, his gleaming boy; every time the benches in Odin's hall creaked, he hoped it was the sound of Balder returning. And Frigg, wretched Frigg, she cried for Balder, she cried for Hod, she cried for everyone.

Nothing would ever be right with this cosmos again.

DEATH BY BLUNDER

THE GODS TAKE VENGEANCE

THE GODS TAKE VENGEANCE

Loki, oh, Loki, Loki, Loki—he just couldn't keep himself from wicked deeds. By tricking Hod into killing Balder, he had caused everyone to grieve. Yet somehow he wound up at a banquet of the Aesir. After all, Loki and Odin were blood brothers, and, truth be told, many had benefited from Loki's deceptions in the past.

This particular banquet was more sumptuous than any other; ale poured into guests' cups without even a servant to hold the flask and the hall was lit by gold rather than flaming tapers. Everyone remarked upon the skills of the two servants who had prepared the banquet: Eldir and Fimafeng. Their work was nothing short of magic. That was enough for Loki; he couldn't bear hearing anyone else praised. So he killed Fimafeng. Just like that. Right there, on sacred ground.

The Aesir drove Loki out into the forest. But Loki came back to the hall, railing against all of them. And Odin was forced to allow him to stay, because of the oath he had once made to always share his drink with Loki. Loki wasn't content just to drink, however. He needed to injure, and so he spewed pain from his lips. He said the goddesses were without virtue, they were trolls in disguise—Idunn and Gefjon and Frigg and Freyja. He accused each god, as well, one after the other, of cowardice—Frey and Tyr and Heimdall and even

PREVIOUS PAGES:
The Aesir held a banquet so sumptuous that ale poured into cups without anyone holding the flask. The servants who had prepared all this received praise, most unfortunately, for them and for envious Loki, as well.

Odin. His ugly words bit like barbs until Thor arrived and threatened to smash Loki with the hammer Mjolnir. Still, Loki spat a final insult before racing away on his long legs into the mountains.

There he built a house with four doors, so that he could look out in all directions to see if anyone was coming. Loki often shape-shifted into a salmon and passed his day in the waterfalls of Franang, flipping through the spray and worrying about who might be coming after him, what that pursuer might be planning. He ripped flax and rolled it between his palms till it formed long threads and he wove a net as he brooded—rolling, weaving, brooding. He'd been doomed from the start ... whose fault was that? Brood, brood.

And then he saw them coming for him.

The Aesir wanted revenge on Loki for causing the death of Balder. So Loki shape-shifted into a fish and swam away while they threw nets and tried to catch him.

Loki dropped his net into the fire and then plunged through the waterfall as a huge salmon.

When the Aesir arrived at the empty hut, the first to enter was the poet Kvasir, who understood things that others didn't, as all poets do. Kvasir took one look at the smoldering net and declared it a fish net. So this posse of Aesir gods quickly spun flax thread and wove a net just like the one that the fire had destroyed. Then they marched down to the stream. Thor held one end of the net and the rest of the Aesir held the other and they cast it wide. It was a good day for fishing.

The net fell near Loki. But Loki swam quickly between two stones, and the net passed above him and came up empty.

The Aesir simply weighted the net. Then they went upstream and cast it again. It was a good day for fishing.

Loki swam fast ahead of that net. It was gaining on him. The deep sea lay ahead, but that sea held too many dangers. So Loki turned and leaped over the net and went back up the waterfalls.

The Aesir saw him leap, of course. So they went after him a third time, starting right at the waterfalls. Now half the

Aesir held one end of the net and the other half held the other end and the strong god Thor waded into the water at the very center of the stream, behind the net, his hands ready, itching to catch the wretched liar Loki. It was a good day for fishing.

Loki swam ahead of the net toward the sea. But he wouldn't venture out into those depths. No. So he turned and leaped again, over the net, right into Thor's hands. Thor carried him by his fish tail into a cavern in the mountains. The Aesir took three large flagstones and bore holes into them and set them end to end. Then they captured two of Loki's sons, Vali and Nari, and they turned Vali into a wolf, who immediately set upon his brother and tore him limb from limb. With Nari's entrails, the gods bound Loki to the three flagstones, a knot at his shoulders, a knot at his hips, a knot at his knees. Instantly, the entrails became iron. The giantess Skadi caught a serpent and fixed him above Loki's

Thor caught Loki and the gods bound him to a rock in a cave. A serpent hung above him dripping poison. Sigyn, one of Loki's wives, caught that poison in a bowl. But whenever she left to empty the bowl, the poison burned Loki.

head, so that venom dripped from the serpent's jaw onto Loki's face. Sigyn, one of Loki's wives, held a basin to catch that poison. But whenever the basin was full to brimming, she had to hurry off to empty it, and in those moments, the poison scalded and ate away at Loki's eyes and nose and lips. Ah, how he screamed and thrashed. The whole cosmos shook. Every earthquake marked the vengeance of the Aesir.

Why did Loki accept this suffering, for surely he did accept it, he must have. He was the shape-shifter supreme. He could have become a flea and slipped out of those knots. But he stayed. Was he just waiting there … waiting for the inevitable, for his chance to play his part in the final conflagration? Or had he somehow given up? Especially after the widening misery he'd caused with Balder's death, had Loki finally come to revile his own trickery? Whatever his motives might have been in accepting the punishment, Loki's very punishment shows how vengeance is a scourge of its own. Think of Vali and Nari. We know little of them. They may have been blameless, guilty of nothing more than being Loki's sons. Guilt by association … is that what the Aesir used to justify the violent undoing of these two men? What a cowardly thing. Perhaps, despite all the wrong motives, Loki was ultimately right in casting aspersions on the characters of the Aesir.

KVASIR'S ENDURING POETRY

In a cosmos with so much violence, the last thing one might expect to thrive was poetry. Yet it did.

At the close of the war between the Aesir and the Vanir, all the gods on both sides spat into a large crock and from that spittle the Aesir made the man Kvasir. This is the same Kvasir that looked upon the net in the fire that Loki had built and recognized it as a fishing net, thus giving the rest of the Aesir information that led to the capture of Loki. Kvasir understood things, and little wonder: He was, after all, made of tiny parts of every god. His very essence was the combination of all their vast knowledge from the beginning of time. Nothing was a mystery to him.

Thus, Kvasir traveled through the cosmos carrying forth his knowledge. Dwarfs, giants, gods all posed him questions. Farmers abandoned their plows, women their salting and sewing, children their chattering, all to gather and listen to Kvasir. If they asked a simple question of fact, he answered forthrightly. But if they asked what they should do, if they wanted his opinion on right or wrong, Kvasir would lean back in his rumpled clothes and let his eyelids slide shut and prod them along. He listened, he nodded, he met questions with questions, and soon they arrived at their own answers. This type of help won him the title of finest poet. And it won him admiration and respect.

And the envy of a pair of brother dwarfs: Fjalar and

PREVIOUS PAGES: The brother dwarfs Fjalar and Galar were envious of the poet Kvasir because he was so admired and respected. They invited him to their cave for a feast—with the very worst of intentions.

Norse Poetry

There were two kinds of poetry in old Norse society. Skaldic poetry was high-style and obeyed complex rules. It was performed at high-status events. Eddic poetry was more straightforward and might occur at gatherings of ordinary folk. But poetry and storytelling, no matter what style, were an important part of communal life. These oral poems and stories recorded historical facts, religious beliefs, and hopes and fears. They gave excitement to nights that might otherwise have seemed interminable.

Odin with his ravens, 18th-century Icelandic manuscript

Galar. They invited Kvasir to feast with them in their underground cave. Though the stalactites dripped chalky-like, and the floor grated under his feet, Kvasir enjoyed the food, especially since it was served on hammered gold plates. After the meal, Fjalar and Galar led the unsuspecting Kvasir into a deeper chamber. They stabbed him and caught his spurting blood in the crocks Son and Bodn and in the kettle Odrorir. Kvasir's huge heart pumped his body dry.

Fjalar and Galar sent word to the Aesir that Kvasir had choked to death on his own knowledge. Then they mixed honey into Kvasir's blood and brewed a mead of which one sip would turn anyone into a poet. The brothers hid the mead away.

A short while later, the giant Gilling and his wife visited these brothers. The giant quarreled with them about this and that,

The wicked brothers Fjalar and Galar killed the giant Gilling. When his wife came looking for him, they said he had drowned in an accident. One ran off to get a millstone to drop on her head and kill her.

and the brothers, incensed, suggested that Gilling might enjoy a sea breeze. So they rowed the giant out into the deep sea surrounding Midgard and slammed the boat into an underwater reef. The boat flipped and the giant drowned. The brothers righted the boat and returned to their cave, where they told Gilling's wife that he had died in an accident. The giantess wept so copiously that the cave was awash with tears. Was there no end to the annoyance of giants? One brother offered to show the wife where Gilling had gone under; the other ran to find a millstone. As Fjalar stood with Gilling's wife on the shore, Galar dropped the millstone on her head.

Gilling and his wife had a son, Suttung, who came looking for them when they didn't return that night. The brothers Fjalar and Galar droned on and on about the sorry accidental deaths of his parents, but Suttung would have none of it. He grabbed them by the scruff of the neck and sloshed with them out to sea, where he fully intended to drop them. It was too long a distance for them to swim back; the brothers were doomed. So they offered Suttung a trade: the magic mead from Kvasir's blood in exchange for their lives. Suttung recognized a good deal when he heard it; after all, his parents were already dead and the joy of vengeance was short-lived at best.

Suttung allowed himself one sip of the brew, and then he put the two crocks and the kettle in a rock box he hewed himself. He hid the box deep in a mountain. He set his daughter Gunnlod to guard it.

Suttung wasn't an entirely smart fellow, however. He bragged about that magic mead far and wide. Word reached Odin—and Odin, we know, had a lust for knowledge. Odin shape-shifted into the form of a giant and called himself Bolverk. He tramped across Midgard until he came to the field that belonged to Baugi, the brother of Suttung. Nine workers were scything the tall grass. The one-eyed Bolverk generously sharpened the thralls' scythes with his whetstone to an edge much finer than any of them had seen before.

The god Odin shape-shifted into a giant. When he came across Baugi's servants in a field, he sharpened their scythes and then threw his whetstone into the air. The servants ran to catch it, slaying each other with their sharpened scythes as they did so.

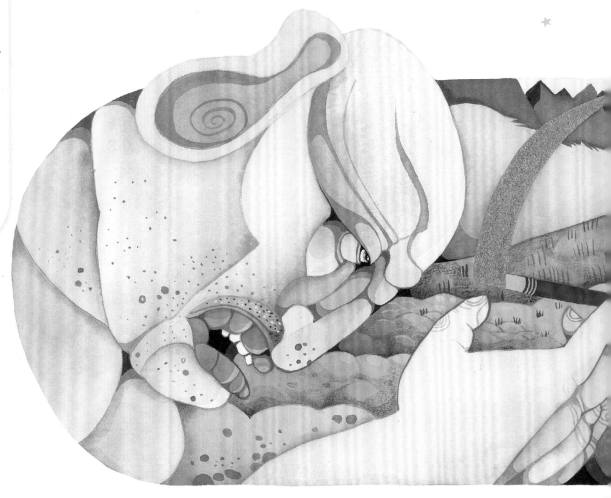

They all wanted to buy that whetstone. Bolverk threw it high and the thralls ran to catch it, bumping into each other in excitement, still holding their newly sharpened scythes. In all that confusion, they ended up slaying each other.

Bolverk wandered on, taking his time. When night finally fell, he went to the home of Baugi and begged for food. Baugi, of course, was beside himself; all his thralls lay dead. He had no one to do the field work. So the one-eyed Bolverk, who was really Odin, offered himself as a field hand, but his price was one sip of the magic mead. Baugi agreed to ask his brother Suttung for the mead. In the meantime, Bolverk worked Baugi's land all summer. When it came time for Bolverk to get his wages, Suttung refused.

So Bolverk enlisted Baugi into helping him steal the mead. And Baugi agreed simply out of fear of this giant who had done the work of nine thralls without shedding a drop of sweat. He led Bolverk to the mountain where the mead was stored and bored a hole into it. Bolverk shape-shifted into a snake and slid through the hole. Baugi tried to gouge him with the auger, but the snake was already gone, into the heart of the mountain.

Gunnlod, Suttung's daughter, moped inside the mountain chamber, desolate and bored, guarding the rock box. Suddenly a giant appeared before her, for Odin the snake had shape-shifted back into Bolverk. Odin in the form of Bolverk sang one of the nine precious songs he had learned when he hung delirious from the sacred tree Yggdrasil. The inexperienced girl was overwhelmed. It was wonderful to have company at last, and it was exquisite to have such handsome male company, who fixed on her only one eye, but such a passionate eye. Besides, who could resist that beguiling song? Gunnlod fell in love. Bolverk asked the besotted girl for three draughts of the mead. With his first gulp, he drained the kettle Odrorir; with his second, the crock Bodn; with his third, the crock Son. Then he shape-shifted into an eagle and flew back toward Asgard.

Suttung saw the eagle overhead and realized at once that the

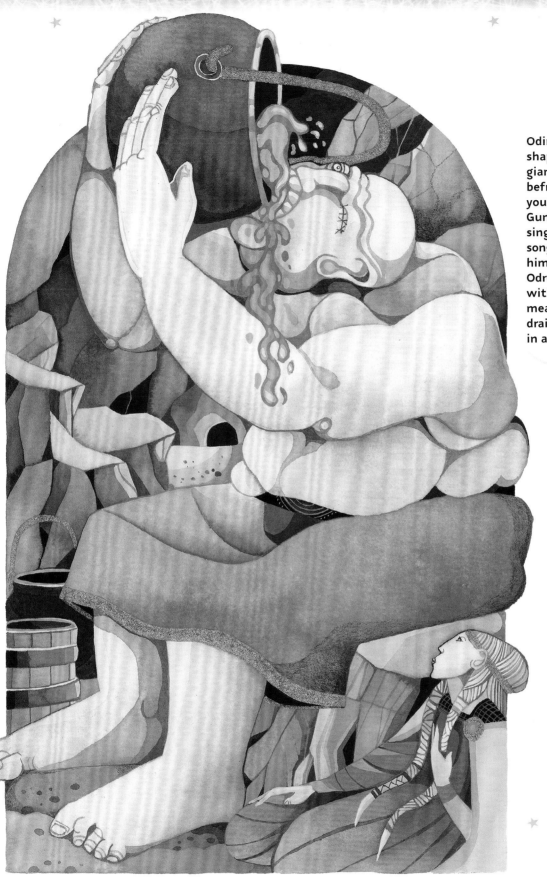

Odin, in the shape of the giant Bolverk, befriended the young giantess Gunnlod by singing a sacred song. She brought him the kettle Odrorir, filled with the magic mead. Odin drained it in a gulp.

Odin filled himself up with the magic mead. Then he shape-shifted into an eagle and flew back to Asgard, with another eagle in chase—the giant Suttung. Odin spewed the mead into pots below, so that Suttung couldn't get it.

mead had been stolen. He murmured enchanted words that he knew only because he had tasted that mead—and thus turned himself into an eagle, too. He flapped after Odin the eagle.

The Aesir saw Odin the eagle coming and they filled the courtyard with bowls and crocks in anticipation of the mead he was bringing. But then they watched a second eagle gain upon the first. They wrung their hands in despair.

Odin the eagle, however, survived; he soared and dove over the wall of Asgard, spewing the mead into the waiting pottery. Some fell outside of the wall, though, and

formed a small pool. Anyone who dared could take a sip, for that was the amateur poets' portion. Odin kept the rest of the mead to himself, and only occasionally offered a draught to a lucky god or man.

The story doesn't end there, though. When the frost giants came to Asgard to find the giant Bolverk who had stolen the mead, Odin proved himself to be as great a liar as Loki; he swore that Bolverk was not there. How the frost giants could look at Odin's one eye and not realize that the one-eyed Bolverk stood before them is a

When he grew up, Bragi, son of Odin and the giantess Gunnlod, had a way with words. He went to live with the Aesir and married Idunn. She carved runes in his tongue to enhance his poetry.

puzzle. Perhaps they understood only what they wanted to understand, for taking on Odin himself would have been formidable. They went back to the grieving Gunnlod with no news.

But Gunnlod must have known the truth in her heart, for she gave birth to a son Bragi, and when the boy was old enough, she sent him to Odin—just as a mother might send her son to his father. The boy was a wordsmith like no other, as though shaped by simply having an origin redolent with the perfumes of that magic mead. Odin made him god of poetry. Bragi married the goddess Idunn, the goddess of the apples that ensure continuing youth. She carved magic runes in her husband's tongue, to help him be a better poet. As a skald—fine poet and storyteller—Bragi gave names to ideas that people had sensed only vaguely until his words clarified and limned them. With his stories, he bragged about the histories of the creatures in this complex cosmos, infusing all with pride in their heritage. His songs gave eternal life to their spirits.

Thus, even in the most thwarted of circumstances, poetry arose and endured, just as it does today no matter where you wander. Suffering and joy—and everything in between—all are fodder for poetry.

DESTRUCTION

DESTRUCTION

Despite poetry, stories, songs, bad things kept happening. Too many bad things, too much mischief, too much sorrow, it all weighed down the cosmos.

Disputes popped up among humans. Ping, ping, ping. Robbers and brutes. Ping, ping, ping. They turned into wars. Bang, clash, boom. This town against that town, neighbors against neighbors, finally the ultimate violation: brothers against brothers, fathers against sons. The sands turned iron. The waters ran red. And it went on and on and on, through one year, the next, the next. The first winter bit at eyes till they teared. The second bit at cheeks till they bled. The third devoured everything and everyone. No summer intervened, just winter blowing into winter blowing into winter, one enormous snow called Fimbulvet. Clouds, storms, ice in a gore-splattered cosmos.

Urdarbrunn, the sacred well where one of Yggdrasil's roots ended, now froze hard, and the burbling, bubbling spring of destiny that welled from it ceased. The very roots of the towering ash rotted, and the dragon Nidhogg finally gnawed through the icy one. The leaves yellowed and fell while the lovely Norns looked on and grieved. The tree shook. It couldn't stop shaking. Creatures everywhere curled in fear.

Firmaments shuddered. Trees swayed till their roots gave up and let them splat to the ground. Boulders tumbled off mountains. Everything burst.

Including all chains. Hel's howling hound, Garm, burst free. Fenrir, the wolf who had bitten off the god Tyr's hand, the wolf who was bound in chains on the island of Lyngvi in the lake Amsvartnir, that vicious son of Loki ran free as well. His trickster father, Loki, trapped in a mountain cavern, tied with the entrails of his own son Nari, festering with hatred toward the Aesir who had devised his torment, that shape-shifter slipped free, squatted like a beast, and then hopped away.

Winds shrieked and waves roared, and still, through all the clamor, three cock crows rang out. Up in Valhalla, the cock Gullinkambi crowed so loud his gold comb nearly shook off. From the bird-wood of the giants, the cock Fjalar crowed a screech as red as his feathers. And down in Hel, the third

Ice & Fire

Hekla volcano, Iceland, 19th century

The Norse migrated to Iceland starting in the mid-800s. They met a harsh land where the interior highlands freeze deep in winter. Those highlands are a desert created by volcanoes. Eighteen of Iceland's 130 volcanoes have been active in the past 1,200 years. When a volcano erupts, ash darkens the sky and coats the land. The lava flow sets trees afire, killing everything in its path. The fires and earth-splitting in the battle of Ragnarok bring to mind a volcanic eruption, don't you think?

At the start of Ragnarok, three cocks crowed; the serpent Jormungand left the sea and rolled across the earth; and the dead came out of Hel and climbed into a boat to go join the horrible battle.

cock crowed to alert the dead. This was it. This was the call to the final battle, Ragnarok. The great conflagration was at last upon them all.

A branch broke off Yggdrasil and struck the serpent Jormungand, who released his own tail and left the sea behind. He rolled like terror upon the earth, writhing his way to the vast field called Vigrid. Fenrir ran beside him to that battlefield, leaving a trail of hungry slobber to match his monstrous brother's trail of venom.

The frost giants, meanwhile, left the land behind and crowded their own terror into a ship and headed for Vigrid. Loki looked around and grimaced. No one was going to have a battle without him! Why, he'd be the leader! Under his command the Aesir would be destroyed. He gathered the dead from Hel and dumped them into a second boat called Naglfar, made of the fingernails and toenails of dead men. They sailed for Vigrid.

The fire giants followed mighty Surt with his flaming sword and tramped over the bridge Bifrost, which cracked under their boots.

Heimdall blew on Gjallarhorn and woke the gods, though how they managed to sleep until now, no one could ever explain. They stumbled together and looked around in bleary confusion, at a total loss. So Odin mounted Sleipnir and

The gods and goddesses and all the fallen warriors who lived in Valhalla and Folkvang put on their armor and went to battle. Odin led the way with his spear, Gungnir.

galloped to the well Mimisbrunn to seek advice from the head of the wise giant Mimir. But what advice was possible? Odin's own sacrificed eye looked out from its hiding spot in the well at all that was, and he knew: Battle was how they had always done things; battle was how they would end things. And so the gods and goddesses and all the fallen warriors that lived in Valhalla and Folkvang put on their breastplates and mail and advanced on Vigrid, Odin at the front holding his spear, Gungnir.

Odin and the wolf Fenrir went straight for each other.

As if that was a signal, the carnage began. The fire giant Surt swung his bright sword at the god Frey. Now was the moment of regret: Frey had given his best of swords to Skirnir in his quest to marry Gerd. All he could do was jam his deer horn through Surt's eye. And so, slash, slash, Surt cut Frey down. Hel's hound, Garm, threw himself at the throat of the god Tyr and both soaked the earth with their blood. Thor killed Jormungand with his hammer, Mjolnir. Then Thor staggered backward, but at the ninth step he, too, fell, vanquished by the venom of the serpent. Loki and Heimdall threw their spears at each other at the same moment; both died. By this time Odin and Fenrir were exhausted, but in a last burst of energy, even with Gungnir stuck deep in his chest, Fenrir stretched his enormous jaws wide and swallowed Odin whole. Odin's son Vidar immediately ripped Fenrir's jaws apart. The wolf lay dead, but so did Odin. The fire giant Surt wielded his flaming sword, setting fire to all even as he sank, blinded and dying from the wounds Frey had inflicted.

When the creatures of the cosmos attacked each other in the battle Ragnarok, the very cosmos was destroyed. Fire engulfed Yggdrasil; winds stole the breath of those still living; and the nine worlds fell into the sea.

From the very beginning of time, the wolf Skoll had snapped and growled behind Sun. Now he caught her. His fangs sank deep. And he swallowed her. Daylight was no more.

The wolf Hati Hrodvitnisson, who had run with lolling tongue after Moon for so very long, seized him and chewed him pitilessly. The night sky went black, not a single star glittered.

All nine worlds swirled with flame; the cosmos was a furnace. Wild winds choked those who yet lived. Yggdrasil fell. The dwarfs' forge tipped and set even that sacred tree afire. One after the other, the nine worlds fell into the sea.

Time ended.

Yet still the earth rose again from the seas—against all odds, yes, but exactly as it had to be. Remember that everything went as fate would have it, all was destined.

DESTRUCTION

Light returned, for Sun had given birth to a daughter as dedicated as she had been, who followed the same path each day. Plants grew, fish swarmed the seas, birds fluttered above. From death came life, just as the first god Bor's three sons carved the cosmos from the corpse of the giant Ymir so long ago, just as spring follows winter.

The god Balder and his brother god Hod, who killed Balder, and their brother god Vali, who killed Hod, all survived and would walk on green grasses without rancor toward anyone. Another of Odin's sons, Vidar, who had avenged his father's death, also lived on, as did Thor's sons Modi and Magni, who kept with them that best of hammers, Mjolnir. And last of the gods to survive was Hoenir, the huge god whose silence cost Mimir his head,

but who now looked at all clearly and foretold the future.
These seven Aesir would rule in the new cosmos.

Two humans had taken refuge inside Yggdrasil, Lif and
Lifthrasir. They would have children and their children
would have children, and they would people the new cosmos
with goodness.

But the dragon Nidhogg survived, too, and with a
purpose. Those who weren't good would die in a cold place,
all doors facing the north wind, all rivers roiling with
poisons. Nidhogg would suck the evil dead dry, till nothing
remained but rattling bones.

Still, this new way would be fair and peaceful.

Ragnarok was the end.

This was the beginning.

The humans Lif and Lifthrasir survived the battle and repeopled the new cosmos. The dragon Nidhogg also survived, and it plagued anyone who was evil. This way, the new beginning promised a fair and peaceful future.

AFTERWORD

The first recorded versions we have of the Norse myths are in Icelandic sagas that date from around A.D. 1180. But somewhere around 1225 the Icelander Snorri, son of Sturla, gave us a major work called the Snorra Edda, also known as Prose Edda. Most of our ideas about Norse mythology today are based on that work.

Many of the Norse texts we have are examples of what is called skaldic poetry, which would have been performed at court events by skilled poets who wrote their own verse. Skaldic poetry obeyed complex rules about internal rhyme, patterns of alliteration, meter, and other issues of stress. The result was often a syntax so convoluted that sometimes scholars are unsure what is actually meant by a given verse.

Snorri offers stories and poems, as well as a poetry handbook that explains the structure of the poems and a prologue that gives a somewhat historical framework for the myths. While Snorri was Christian, he treats the pagan mythology with respect. Some of the Icelandic sagas were probably written by Snorri, but others were written after his death, well into the 14th century. The Prose Edda was preserved in the manuscript called Codex Regius 2367, 4Ð.

Alongside Snorri's work is another collection, called the Poetic Edda. It is preserved in the manuscript Codex Regius 2364, 4Ð. It contains a

This is an illustration from an Icelandic manuscript of the 18th century. Here the god Heimdall is blowing Gjallarhorn to summon the Aesir to a meeting.

collection of poems in a much more relaxed form, the style of which has become known as Eddic. These poems were anonymous and performed by all sorts of people on all sorts of occasions; they are clear and easily comprehensible.

As I was writing this book, I consulted translations of both works and I came across a number of inconsistencies between the mythological tales. The inconsistencies I found are of three types, and the way I handled them in this book varies based on the type.

One type is logical inconsistency. Since the reader is very likely to pick up on this, I face it head-on. In "The Gods Take Revenge" Loki is bound up till the conflagration of Ragnarok. But Loki is a shape-shifter. He could easily have turned into a flea and escaped. The sources I consulted did not address this inconsistency. So I mention it at the end of the chapter as a question for the reader. Other times characters behave as though they don't know the future, when, in fact, they should. In "Death by Blunder," for example, Loki disguises himself as an old woman and asks Frigg if any object in the cosmos failed to take the oath not to harm Balder. Frigg knows the future, so she should either not answer Loki or be tied up in knots by not being able to stop herself from answering him, fully aware of what he'll do with the information. Instead, she seems to simply answer him as though she has no idea what will come of it. So I question her behavior right there in the chapter.

A second problem is inconsistencies of facts. For example, in "Idunn's Apples" Odin and Loki and Hoenir are hungry and can't get meat to cook over an open fire because an eagle has put a magic spell on it. Odin's mouth waters for this meat. But Odin is supposed to live on wine alone. There was no way to address this inconsistency without breaking dramatic momentum. In my retelling, therefore, I simply don't mention Odin's feelings about the meat in order not to confront the reader with a conflict that to me seems irrelevant. For another, Odin's brothers are called Vili and Ve in the Poetic Edda, but later we find that three gods brought humans to life: Odin, Hoenir, and Lodur. In the Prose Edda those three gods are said to be sons of Bor. But nowhere does it say that Bor had more than three sons. I didn't want to leave out the names of the three gods who were so important to the origin of humans, so I simply said the number of gods had grown and I didn't bring up whether these particular three gods were brothers or not. Likewise, one of Odin's sons and one of Loki's sons share the name Vali, and scholars point out potential confusions between the two. But I simply left both gods with the name given them in the Poetic Edda and made sure to make it clear each time I discussed them which one was involved. And, finally, the name Fjalar in this book belongs to a dwarf and to a rooster. Actually, it was a common name in Norse mythology for any deceiver, so it might not have been a name at all but an epithet (like naming someone Liar).

A third kind of inconsistency involves time. When Loki is insulting everyone at the feast in the huge hall in "The Gods Take Revenge," he includes in his harangue Bragi, the god of poetry. Soon after this, Kvasir helps to trap Loki. But Bragi is not born until after Kvasir's death. Here I resolve the issue by simply not mentioning Bragi in the list of gods that Loki insults, since Bragi does not take any action of note at this

feast—so no inconsistency slaps the reader in the face. Another possible inconsistency is in "Frey & Gerd," when Skirnir offers Gerd the ring Draupnir if she'll marry Frey. This is

This is an illustration from an Icelandic manuscript of the 17th century. Here we see Valhalla on one side and Jormungand on the other.

based on the poem "Skírnismál" of the Poetic Edda, and it is unclear where this event fits among the others timewise. To me, for dramatic effect, this story should immediately follow the story of Skadi and Njord, so that's where I put it. But the ring presents a problem. The dwarf Brokk gave Draupnir to Odin. At Balder's funeral, Odin, distraught with grief, threw it into the blazing ship that was his son's coffin. But later, when Hermod went to Hel to try to win Balder's freedom, Balder gave Draupnir to Hermod and asked him to return it to Odin. I don't know how it came to be in Skirnir's hands at any point. But, perhaps, if Skirnir has Draupnir, then Loki is dead. Yet at this point in my retelling, Loki is still alive. I try to allay any confusions the reader might have by saying it's anyone's guess how the ring fell into Skirnir's hands.

This third kind of inconsistency is interesting. I have found time inconsistencies repeatedly in mythologies of many cultures, including those of ancient Greece and ancient Egypt. This may be partially due to the fact that different people wrote down the different tales and at different times, and may not have been aware of (or cared to dovetail with) what the others wrote—leading to inconsistencies. And certainly, traditional stories often have multiple variants. But it might also suggest that mythologies sometimes do not adhere to linear chronology. Why can't time simply fold back on itself, especially in a world riddled with magic?

THE ANCIENT NORSE WORLD

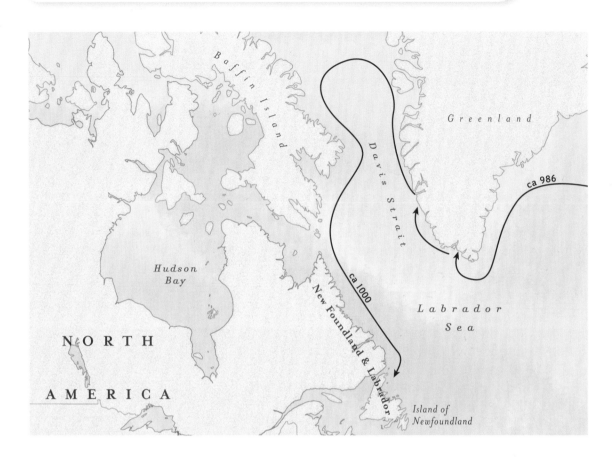

TIME LINE OF NORSE HISTORY

8000–4000 B.C.
The glaciers gradually retreat, allowing humans to inhabit Scandinavia.

Circa 4000 B.C.
Hunting tribes follow reindeer into southern Scandinavia. They are ancestors of the Sami people (who live north of the Arctic Circle today). Petroglyphs (rock drawings) date back to this time.

Circa 1550 B.C.
Tribes settle central Sweden and western Norway. Traders travel inland rivers from the Baltic Sea down to the Mediterranean on a path known as the Amber Route, since amber was a valuable commodity of the north.

1000 B.C.
Indo-European tribes settle in Scandinavia; the proto-Germanic language develops its own characteristics.

500 B.C.
The Iron Age begins in Scandinavia through contact with the La Tène Celtic civilization to the south.

450–50 B.C.
Scandinavians trade heavily with Celts, who occupy most of Europe in competition with Greeks and Romans.

200 B.C.
Scandinavian tribes move into Germany and eastern Europe, displacing Celts, many of whom move into the British Isles and Ireland. The north branch of proto-Germanic begins to form Old Norse.

Early times– A.D. 150
Around 3000 B.C. people in Denmark used planks to build up the edges of canoes. Circa 2000 to 500 B.C. boats developed high posts at each end with prows depicting dragon heads or other animals. By A.D. 100–150 boats had become long, with planks, ribs, and end posts of oak, and a wide middle area that had a mast and sail. Long oars were looped to rowlocks. They were fast and agile.

150 B.C.
The first runes we know of date to 150 B.C. They were found in Denmark and northern Germany. The runes were letters evolved from Old Italic alphabets carved into stones. Their uses are a mystery; perhaps they named tribes, perhaps they were magical signs.

Circa 120 B.C.
Romans settle throughout Europe. Around 58–51 B.C., Scandinavian tribes, known as Goths, move from Sweden into central Europe. By 25 B.C. the Danes of Jutland are trading heavily with western Europe.

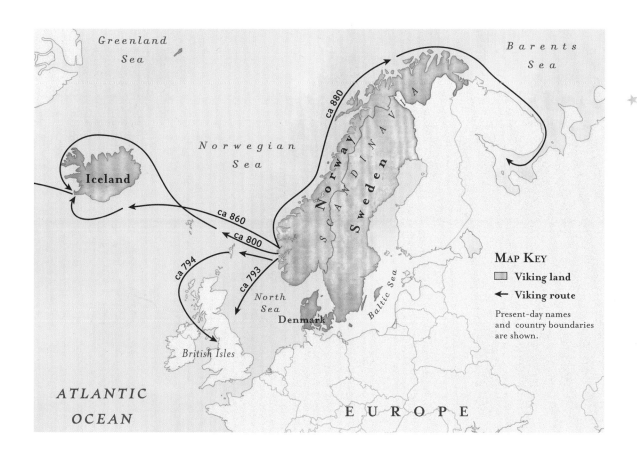

Circa A.D. 325–500

Christianity spreads via Romans to Goths in central Europe. Tribes skirmish, especially Germanic and Roman. Pirates plague the seas. The Huns, nomads of central Asia, the Caucasus mountains, and eastern Europe, under the leadership of Attila, conquer much of eastern Germanic lands between A.D. 433 and 452. Attila the Hun greatly weakens the influence of Romans. By A.D. 476 the Western Roman Empire collapses.

Circa A.D. 450–650

West Germanic tribes, including from Jutland, invade and settle in the British Isles.

Circa A.D. 550–790

Uppsala, the eastern central part of Sweden, becomes a major economic force. It exports iron, fur, and slaves. Its horses are renowned for strength and speed.

Circa A.D. 500–1160

The Danes build the wall Danevirke across southern Jutland to keep out Frankish tribes from the south. (Written sources say construction began in 808. But carbon dating in 2013 shows construction began before A.D. 500.)

A.D. 772–785

In 772 Charlemagne, ruler of the Frankish Kingdom (most of western Europe), starts a campaign to exterminate non-Christians, including the Norse. In 778–785 the Danes assist the Saxons in their resistance to Charlemagne.

Circa A.D. 790–1066

This is the Viking age. Vikings raid England, Scotland, and Ireland, and then also Spain, France, Wales, and Germany. From 848 to 871 Norwegians fight Danes for control of Ireland. Circa 860 the Norse discover Iceland; ten years later they settle there. In 878 Alfred the Great forces Christianity on the Danes; many Danes and Norwegians flee to Iceland. In 912 Vikings take over the northern Frankish lands, which thereafter is called Normandy. In 947 Norway adopts Christianity; soon Denmark does the same. In 982 Erik the Red discovers Greenland; four years later Vikings settle there. In 1000 Iceland converts to Christianity. Circa 1000 Leif Eriksson discovers North America, but the native people fight him off. In the first half of the 1000s Normans (who are of Norse descent, but French-speaking) invade Italy and Sicily. In 1066 Normans take over England. After this point there are no more "Viking" invasions, and belief in the old gods withers.

Name: BALDER

Norse name: Baldr

Known for: being as sweet as he was handsome, being killed by his brother Hod

Lineage: son of Frigg and Odin

Married to: Nanna

Name: FENRIR

Norse name: Fenrir

Known for: biting off the hand of Odin's son Tyr, killing Odin at final battle of Ragnarok

Lineage: wolf son of Loki and the frost giantess Angrboda

Married to: unknown

Name: BROKK AND SINDRI

Norse name: Brokk and Sindri

Known for: making Thor's hammer, Mjolnir, and Odin's ring, Draupnir

Lineage: dwarf brothers

Married to: unknown

Name: FREY

Norse name: Frey

Known for: being god of fertility of the land

Lineage: son of Njord, twin of Freyja

Married to: Gerd

Name: BURI

Norse name: Búri

Known for: being the first god, father of Bor, grandfather of Odin

Lineage: the cow Audhumla licked him free from the ice

Married to: unknown, but probably a frost giantess

Name: FREYJA

Norse name: Freyja

Known for: beauty, wearing a falcon-feather cloak

Lineage: daughter of Njord, twin of Frey

Married to: Od, who disappeared

Name: FRIGG

Norse name: Frigg

Known for: foreknowledge, being the mother of Balder and Hod

Lineage: Aesir goddess

Married to: Odin

Name: HEL

Norse name: Hel

Known for: presiding over those who die of sickness or old age

Lineage: daughter of Loki and the frost giantess Angrboda

Married to: never married

Name: GERD

Norse name: Gerð

Known for: beauty

Lineage: daughter of giant Gymir

Married to: Frey

Name: HOD

Norse name: Höð

Known for: being blind, being tricked into killing his brother Balder

Lineage: son of Frigg and Odin

Married to: unknown

Name: HEIMDALL

Norse name: Heimdall

Known for: guarding the entrance to Asgard and being progenitor of the classes of people

Lineage: son of Odin

Married to: unknown

Name: IDUNN

Norse name: Iðunn

Known for: apples that keep the gods young and strong

Lineage: Aesir goddess

Married to: Bragi

Name: JORMUNGAND

Norse name: Jörmungand

Known for: circling Midgard and killing Thor at final battle of Ragnarok

Lineage: serpent son of Loki and the frost giantess Angrboda

Married to: unknown

Name: MIMIR

Norse name: Mímir

Known for: wisdom and memory, having his head severed by the Vanir

Lineage: giant, perhaps the brother of Odin's mother, Bestla

Married to: Sinmara

Name: KVASIR

Norse name: Kvasir

Known for: knowledge and poetry

Lineage: born from the spit of the Aesir and Vanir gods

Married to: unknown

Name: NJORD

Norse name: Njörð

Known for: wisdom, love of boats and harbors

Lineage: Vanir god, traded to the Aesir with twin son and daughter

Married to: Skadi

Name: LOKI

Norse name: Loki

Known for: shape-shifting, troublemaking

Lineage: son of the giant Farbauti and the goddess Laufey

Married to: at least three wives

Name: ODIN

Norse name: Óðinn

Known for: one eye, wisdom, ruling Asgard

Lineage: son of Bor and Bestla

Married to: Frigg

Name: SKADI

Norse name: Skaði

Known for: zipping over the frozen countryside on skis

Lineage: daughter of the giant Thjazi

Married to: Njord

Name: THOR

Norse name: Þórr

Known for: his hammer, Mjolnir; fierce fighting

Lineage: son of Odin and the earth

Married to: Sif

Name: SKIRNIR

Norse name: Skírnir

Known for: being the servant and messenger of Frey

Lineage: unknown

Married to: unknown

Name: THRYM

Norse name: Þrym

Known for: using Thor's hammer as ransom to demand Freyja as his wife

Lineage: king of the frost giants

Married to: unknown

Name: SKRYMIR

Norse name: Skrýmir

Known for: his giant glove that Thor and his men slept in

Lineage: giant king of Jotunheim

Married to: unknown

Name: VALKYRIES

Norse name: Valkyrja

Known for: carrying wounded soldiers to Valhalla

Lineage: unknown

Married to: some did marry

Below I list the works I consulted. I tip my hat with admiration to Kevin Crossley-Holland, whose lyricism is unrivaled.

The quote "Cattle die" in "Odin's Quest" is from the first section of the poem "Hávamál," as translated in Abram (2011: page 104).

References

Abram, Christopher. *Myths of the Pagan North: The Gods of the Norsemen.* New York: Continuum International Publishing Group, 2011.

Brancaleoni, Greta, Elena Nikitenkova, Luigi Grassi, and Vidje Hansen. "Seasonal Affective Disorder and Latitude of Living." *Epidemiologia e Psichiatra Sociale* 18, no. 4 (2009): 336-343.

Brodeur, Arthur Gilchrist (trans.). *The Prose Edda,* by Snorri Sturluson. New York and London: Oxford University Press, 1916. Available at: http://books.google.com/books?id=Ls2F5i6_LeYC&printsec=frontcover&dq=prose+edda%23v=onepage&q=&f=false#v=onepage&q&f=false.

Brown, Nancy Marie. *Song of the Vikings: Snorri and the Making of Norse Myths.* New York: MacMillan, 2012.

Byock, Jesse (trans.). *The Prose Edda.* London: Penguin Books, 2006.

Chisholm, James Allen. "The Eddas: The Keys to the Mysteries of the North." http://www.heathengods.com/library/poetic_edda/ChisholmEdda.pdf (accessed November 3, 2013).

Conover, David O. "Adaptive Significance of Temperature-Dependent Sex Determination in a Fish." *American Naturalist* (1984): 297-313.

Crossley-Holland, Kevin. *The Norse Myths.* New York: Pantheon, 1980.

Davidson, Hilda Roderick Ellis. *Gods and Myths of Northern Europe.* London: Penguin, 1964. Partially available at: http://www.amazon.com/Myths-Northern-Europe-Ellis-Davidson/dp/0140136274 and at http://www.faqs.org/faqs/nordic-faq/part2_NORDEN/section-3.html.

Dennis, Andrew, Peter Foote, and Richard Perkins (trans.). *Laws of Early Iceland.* Grágás II. Winnipeg: University of Manitoba Press, 2000.

Dronke, Ursula (ed. & trans.). *The Poetic Edda.* Vol. I, *Heroic Poems.* Oxford, UK: Clarendon, 1969.

Dronke, Ursula (ed. & trans.). *The Poetic Edda.* Vol. II, *Mythological Poems.* Oxford, UK: Clarendon, 1997.

Dumézil, Georges. *Gods of the Ancient Northmen.* Ed. Einar Haugen. Berkeley: University of California Press, 1973.

Einarsdóttir, Katrín Sif. "The Role of Horses in the Old Norse Sources: Transcending Worlds, Mortality and Reality." Doctoral dissertation, University of Iceland (2013).

Faulkes, Anthony (ed. & trans.). *Edda by Snorri Sturluson.* London: Orion House, 1987.

Grimes, Heilan Yvette. *The Norse Myths.* Boston: Hollow Earth Publishing, 2010.

Helgason, Agnar, Sigrun Sigurðar-dottir, Jayne Nicholson, Bryan Sykes, Emmeline W. Hill, Daniel G. Bradley, Vidar Bosnes, Jeffery R. Gulcher, Ryk Ward, and Kári Stefánsson. "Estimating Scandi-navian and Gaelic Ancestry in the Male Settlers of Iceland." *American Journal of Human Genetics* 67, no. 3 (2000): 697-717.

Hewitt, Julia Cuervo. *Voices Out of Africa in the Twentieth-Century Spanish Caribbean Literature.* Cranbury, NJ: Rosemont Publishing & Printing Corp, 2009.

Hollander, Lee M. (trans.) *The Poetic Edda.* Austin: University of Texas Press, 1962.

Hollander, Lee M. (trans.). *The Poetic Edda: Translated With an Introduction and Explanatory Notes,* (2nd ed., rev.). Austin: University of Texas Press, 2010.

Huntford, Roland. *Two Planks and a Passion: The Dramatic History of Skiing.* London: Continuum Interna-tional Publishing Group, 2008.

Jesch, Judith. *Women in the Viking Age.* Woodbridge, Suffolk, UK: Boydell & Brewer Ltd., 1991.

Jones, Gwyn. *A History of the Vikings.* Oxford, UK: Oxford University Press, 2001.

Larrington, Carolyne (trans.). *The Poetic Edda.* Oxford, UK: Oxford University Press, 1996.

McDonald, Russell Andrew, and Angus A. Somerville (eds.). *The Viking Age: A Reader.* Vol. 14. Toronto: University of Toronto Press, 2010.

McKinnell, John. "Myth as Therapy: The Usefulness of Þrymskvida." *Medium Ævum* 69, no. 1 (2000): 1-20.

Munch, Peter Andreas. *Norse Mythology: Legends of Gods and Heroes, In the Revision of Magnus Olsen.* (original, 1927). Translated from the Norwegian by Sigurd Bernhard Hustvedt. New York: The American-Scandinavian Foundation, 1963.

Policansky, David. "Sex Change in Plants and Animals." *Annual Review of Ecology and Systematics* 13 (1982): 471-495.

Sawyer, Peter Hayes (ed.). *The Oxford Illustrated History of the Vikings.* Oxford, UK: Oxford University Press, 2001.

Shojaei, Bahador, Reza Kheiran-dish, and Mohammad Hasanzade. "Monocephalus Tetrapus Dibra-chius in a Calf." *Comparative Clinical Pathology* 19, no. 5 (2010): 511-513.

Sørensen, Preben Meulengracht. "Þórr's Fishing Expedition" [Hymiskviða] [tf. Kirsten Williams], in *The Poetic Edda: Essays on Old Norse Mythology,* eds. Paul Acker and Carolyne Larrington. New York and London: Routledge, 2002: 119-138.

Spence, Lewis. *An Introduction to Mythol-ogy.* New York: Cosimo, Inc., 2004.

Tarqum, Steven, and Norman Rosenthal. "Seasonal Affective Disorder." *Psychiatry* 5, no. 5 (2008): 31-33.

Varner, Gary R. *Sacred Wells: A Study in the History, Meaning, and Mythology of Holy Wells & Waters.* New York: Algora Publishing, 2009.

INDEX

For Barry, il mio vichingo. —DJN

For my very dear friend Joe Boyle …
a Norse traveler if ever there was one. —CB

Enormous gratitude for guidance throughout this project goes to Professor Scott Mellor of the Department of Scandinavian Studies at the University of Wisconsin at Madison. The author and illustrator also thank the National Geographic team who worked on this project for their resourcefulness, energy, and wisdom: Amy Briggs, Priyanka Lamichhane, Hillary Leo, and David Seager.

Staff for This Book

Priyanka Sherman and Amy Briggs, *Senior Editors*
David M. Seager, *Art Director and Designer*
Callie Broaddus, *Associate Designer*
Hillary Leo, *Photo Editor*
Carl Mehler, *Director of Maps*
Paige Towler, *Editorial Assistant*
Sanjida Rashid and Rachel Kenny,
   Design Production Assistants
Michael Cassady, *Rights Clearance Specialist*
Grace Hill, *Managing Editor*
Mike O'Connor, *Production Editor*
Lewis R. Bassford, *Production Manager*
Rachel Faulise, *Manager, Production Services*
Susan Borke, *Legal and Business Affairs*

Senior Management Team, Kids Publishing and Media

Nancy Laties Feresten, *Senior Vice President*
Jennifer Emmett, *Vice President, Editorial Director, Kids Books*
Julie Vosburgh Agnone, *Vice President, Editorial Operations*
Rachel Buchholz, *Editor and Vice President, NG Kids magazine*
Michelle Sullivan, *Vice President, Kids Digital*
Eva Absher-Schantz, *Design Director*
Jay Sumner, *Photo Director*
Hannah August, *Marketing Director*
R. Gary Colbert, *Production Director*

Digital

Anne McCormack, *Director*
Laura Goertzel, Sara Zeglin, *Producers*
Emma Rigney, *Creative Producer*
Bianca Bowman, *Assistant Producer*
Natalie Jones, *Senior Product Manager*

ILLUSTRATIONS CREDITS

All illustrations: Christina Balit.
Photos: 13 (INSET), Vito Palmisano/Getty Images; 21 (INSET), filmfoto/Shutterstock; 31 (INSET), Werner Forman Archive/Statens Historiska Museum, Stockholm/Heritage-Images/Art Resource, NY; 41 (INSET), Ko Backpacko/Shutterstock; 47 (INSET), Oldmantravels/Flickr; 55 (INSET), Werner Forman Archive/Statens Historiska Museum, Stockholm/Heritage-Images/Art Resource, NY; 63 (INSET), Detail of figures illustrating a saga, from the Isle of Gotland (stone) by Viking (9th century), Historiska Museet, Stockholm, Sweden/Bridgeman Images; 71 (INSET), David Robertson/Alamy; 71 (INSET BACK), Chanwut Jukrachai/Shutterstock; 79 (INSET), The Market of Tlatelolco, detail from the Great City of Tenochtitlan, from the cycle "Pre-Hispanic and Colonial Mexico," 1945 (mural) (see also 97395), Rivera, Diego (1886–1957)/Palacio Nacional, Mexico City, Mexico/Bridgeman Images; 87 (INSET), Shutterstock; 95 (INSET), © Juan Carlos Munoz/Robert Harding World Imagery; 105 (INSET), Fedorov Oleksiy/Shutterstock; 115 (INSET), Soldiers for the Norwegian King Sverre, Torstein Skevla and Skjervald Skrukka carrying the king's son Hakon Hakonsson, 1869 (oil on canvas)/Bridgeman Images; 125 (INSET), simonekesh/Shutterstock; 133 (INSET), Henrik Larsson/Shutterstock; 143 (INSET), Jason Steel/Shutterstock; 151 (INSET), Odin, with his two crows, Hugin (thought) and Munin (memory) (pen & ink on paper), Icelandic School (18th century)/Royal Library, Copenhagen, Denmark/Bridgeman Images; 165 (INSET), NMPFT/Science Museum/SSPL/Getty Images; 174, Heimdall Blowing His Horn Before Ragnarok, from "Melsted's Edda" (pen & ink and w/c on paper), Icelandic School (18th century)/Arni Magnusson Institute, Reykjavik, Iceland/Bridgeman Images; 178, Valhalla and the Midgard Serpent, 1680, Icelandic School (17th century)/Arni Magnusson Institute, Reykjavik, Iceland/Bridgeman Images

Library of Congress Cataloging-in-Publication Data

Napoli, Donna Jo, 1948- author.
Treasury of Norse mythology : stories of intrigue, trickery, love, and revenge
/ by Donna Jo Napoli ; illustrated by Christina Balit.
pages cm
Audience: Ages 8-12
Includes bibliographical references and index.
ISBN 978-1-4263-2098-9 (hardcover : alk. paper) -- ISBN 978-1-4263-2099-6 (library binding : alk. paper)
1. Mythology, Norse--Juvenile literature. 2. Gods, Norse--Juvenile literature. 3. Tales--Scandinavia. I. Balit, Christina, illustrator. II. Title.
BL860.N25 2015
398.209368--dc23

Printed in China
18/RRDS/2

Cover: *Four inhabitants of Asgard: Odin on his throne, two wolves at his feet; stunning Freyja in her falcon-feather coat; Thor with his hammer high, ready to bash enemies; and Loki lurking, envious and spiteful*